REVELATION:
THE PASSOVER KEY

An Interpretation of the Book of Revelation

REVELATION:
THE PASSOVER KEY

An Interpretation of the Book of Revelation

Daniel C. Juster

With Preface and Appendix by
Keith Intrater

Destiny Image Publishers
P.O. Box 351
Shippensburg, PA 17257-0351

"Speaking to the Purposes of God
for this Generation"

Tikkun Ministries
P.O. Box 7538
Gaithersburg, MD 20898-7538

ISBN 1-56043-044-3

For Worldwide Distribution
Printed in the U.S.A.

Table of Contents

Table of Contents

Preface

Dan Juster's insights into the Book of Revelation offer several advantages to the reader. First, Dan is a widely read scholar who is well versed in many streams of church thought and theology. When he explains a text from Revelation, he is taking into consideration the various ways the text has been interpreted throughout history. This gives the reader the benefit of a *broad-based analysis* without having to do all the background research.

Secondly, Dan uses the story of the Passover as a key to understanding the highly symbolic and complicated language of the Book of Revelation. The comparisons of pharaoh with the Antichrist, the plagues of Exodus with the plagues of Revelation and the Red Sea victory with Armageddon, among others, help to simplify and make sense of the overall meaning of the end-times prophecies.

The application of Old Testament symbolism to Revelation is the correct approach to understanding the symbolism there.

Finally, Dan's experience as a pastor leads him to draw practical applications from the Book of Revelation that will help believers live by faith in these end times. Ultimately, the Passover led to great victory for God's people. So will the events of the Book of Revelation culminate in the manifestation of God's Kingdom on earth. As the Israelites in Goshen were protected from the plagues, so will the faithful saints of the end times be sealed and protected by God's power.

Dan's unique combination of scholarship, Messianic theology and practical pastoring gives us a perspective on the Book of Revelation that is truly eye-opening. It will help to prepare you for Jesus' imminent return. Read and enjoy.

Keith Intrater, Pastor
Beth Messiah Congregation
Gaithersburg, MD

Introduction and Background

This book is intended to be a general introduction to the Book of Revelation. It does not pretend to be an exhaustive interpretive commentary. It is not our purpose to interpret each verse or to identify every symbol, event and numerical prediction. It is rather our intent to provide a key that will open up a broad, inspiring and practical understanding of the book. The literature on the Book of Revelation contains many varied interpretations of the particulars found within the book. Some of these variations are compatible interpretations and applications. Others are ultimately incompatible. Some are convincing, while others are farfetched. I believe that the Passover-Exodus key to the Book of Revelation provides us with the best overall understanding for evaluating various approaches. The Book of Revelation is notoriously difficult to interpret. A few years ago, the late Dean of the Graduate School at Wheaton College, Dr. Merrill Tenney, published a book entitled *Interpreting Revelation*. This is a very fine work for the student who wishes to gain a better grasp of the book. I believe most interpretations of Revelation use one or a combination of the approaches outlined in Dr. Tenney's book. They are as follows.

The Symbolic Approach: This approach looks to the book primarily to gain insight into the nature of spiritual opposition and struggle at all times and for all believers. Through this method, all believers undergoing persecution or duress may be encouraged toward the ultimate victory of Jesus and His Kingdom. Those of this school shun historical, or prophetic past or future identifications for the symbols and content of the book.

The Preterist Approach: This approach views the book as presenting the spiritual struggle of the first century believers with the Roman Empire and Jewish opposition. It is believed that the prophetic content of the book is fully past, excepting the literal return of Jesus the Messiah.

The Historical Approach: This approach sees the book as representing the progress of history from the time of the Ascension of Jesus the Messiah until His second coming and the establishment of the New Jerusalem. Days and calculations in the book are seen as symbolic of years.

The Futurist Approach: This approach sees the book, especially after chapter four, as representing the last great tribulation before the return of Jesus.

These approaches to Revelation are used by people of widely differing theological persuasions. However, most Futurists are Pre-Millennialists, believing that a literal 1000-year Millennial Age of peace on earth (Revelation 20) precedes the full establishment of the new heavens and earth. There are, however, many who use the historical approach who believe in a literal Millennium. Most of those who believe that there is no literal Millennium, but that the Millennium of chapter 20 is symbolic of this Church Age, are not Futurists, but hold to one or a combination of the first three views.

Augustine was the most famous interpreter of the Symbolic school. The famous fourth century mystic and theologian saw Revelation as repeating seven cycles which said the same thing in varying terms. Each cycle shows the nature of spiritual warfare during this age and ends with the reign of Jesus. Hence the seals, trumpets and bowls of wrath cover the same period of time. The Millennium of chapter 20 also covers that same period. However, it provides the perspective of the rule of the saints from heaven during this age.

The Reformers after Luther saw the Book of Revelation in historical terms. They saw the Pope himself as the clearest revelation of the meaning of the Antichrist. They identified plagues and struggles in the book as connected to events throughout history. Others combine the Reformed tradition with the Preterist persuasion. This is especially so for those who believe that the Church will conquer all obstacles and rule the whole world for a thousand years (Revelation 20) before Jesus the Messiah returns. Thus they would not be expecting any future Antichrist to necessarily arise. Indeed, the Olivet discourse of Matthew 24, Luke 21 and Mark 13 are all seen as referring to the events of the first century; most of the Book of Revelation is seen as having been completed during period of the the Roman Empire.

There is significant truth in each of these approaches. Rare is that teacher who does not teach his view dogmatically. The student of the Word is shaken as he hears one forceful presentation after another, but finds them to be contradictory. Yet all of these interpretations contain truth.

The Symbolic approach recognizes that the Book of Revelation is to have immediate relevance to the spiritual struggle of the persecuted Church in any age. All interpreters recognize that the book is full of symbol and metaphor. However, this school shuns specific identifications of past, present and future events so that believers of any time might see themselves in terms of the spiritual warfare presented in this book. Every generation is to see themselves as perhaps the last generation before Jesus returns. Hence this symbolic approach will seem most awesomely true for the last generation of this transitional age. I believe that this interpretation is very important and provides true application for believers, especially those under great trials. This is the approach taken in Earl Paulk's *Ultimate Kingdom*. I wrote a preface to that volume noting its validity in these regards. It is the best presentation of these truths for the believer in his present struggles of which I am aware. At the same time, as I wrote, I tried to make it clear that I believe in a last days interpretation with specific applications to Israel, which is yet crucial to me.

The Preterist approach is important because it calls us to fully see the background of the book. Certainly the worship-demanding Roman emperor was an antichrist. The book's seven hills unmistakably point to the seven hills of Rome. I believe John's prophecy made more sense to the first and second century believers than to any other generation in history. However, I believe it will have more immediate meaning for those alive just before the coming of the Lord. It will more exactly fit them than even the first century community. The last days' people of God will find themselves, more than any other generation, in the situation most closely paralleling that of the early Church.

The Historical approach is helpful in showing that throughout history there have been many events and situations that parallel the content of the book. Yet it also gives a vivid sense that we are closer to the Lord's appearing than any previous generation.

As will be seen throughout this book, my approach, though having sympathy with some of the features of each approach, is most oriented toward that of *the Futurist*. I do believe that parts of Revelation span this entire age. However, I believe that some parts will find their greatest fulfillment in events yet to take place upon the earth.

My approach to the Book of Revelation is not only the product of study, but I believe it was given to me by revelation from the Spirit of God. I do not expect you, the reader, to simply accept this claim. However, if the interpretation put forth here is true to the evidence and powerfully opens the book to you, I would encourage you to see this approach as from the Lord.

About two years before the writing of this Introduction, I believe the Lord spoke to me: **"If you want to understand the Book of Revelation, the key is the Passover and Exodus from Egypt." Spirit-inspired reflection upon this word gave me a dramatic sense that the Book of Revelation was most relevant to the** generation that would be alive before the return of Jesus and that the events of the Revelation parallel the Exodus events in amazing ways.

The people of God in the last days are a counterpart to the Jews at the time of the Exodus. Antichrist and his system parallel Pharaoh and the Egyptian system. Some biblical scholars have noted Passover-Exodus similarities in the Book of Revelation. However, I do not know of any who have used Passover-Exodus as a total interpretive key for the last days' people of God. As can be seen from this comment, I believe the Body of the Messiah is involved with the events of this book throughout, not absent from them, and looking down at the tribulation from heaven. How this relates to Israel is yet to be brought out in the content of this book.

The Kingdom of God

Before we begin to look into the text itself, I believe that it is important to clarify the meaning of the New Testament concept of the Kingdom of God and how it relates to the Book of Revelation. As some readers are aware, the concept of the Kingdom is quite controversial today, especially to those involved in the Charismatic Movement. This is especially true regarding what is being dubbed by its critics the *Kingdom Now Movement.* This is a movement of Charismatics that emphasizes the preaching of the Gospel of the Kingdom. However, theologies among those in this movement show vast differences. Furthermore, there is no unifying authority structure among these groups. For many, the Kingdom Movement simply represents the discovery by Charismatics of emphases that were widely taught in Reformed theology (by Luther, Calvin and others). It is a departure from the theology of J. N. Darby as represented in the *Scofield Reference Bible.* These emphases are now combined with Charismatic giftings and power.

Kingdom people believe (as is taught by George Ladd) that the Gospel includes principles that are to have an impact on every area of life. Wherever the rule of God is manifested, whether in healings, deliverance from demons, healing family relationships or starting an alternative school system, we see a manifestation of the Kingdom of God. The Kingdom of God came in the ministry of Jesus and continues to be shown in the ministry of the Church and of believers who affect every area of life. Hence the Gospel of the Kingdom is the good news of the opportunity to come under the rule of God and to see every area of life impacted by the power and principles of God. This is a contrast to the teaching of Scofield and Darby, which said that the manifestation of the Kingdom of God was postponed when Israel rejected Jesus. This postponement included the view that the Church does not even preach the Gospel of the Kingdom today, but rather the Gospel of the grace of God, that is, the way of accepting Jesus as Savior. It is taught that only after the Church has been raptured before the tribulation will the saved of Israel again preach the Gospel of the Kingdom.

Some Kingdom people (a minority, to be sure) hold that the Church will so extend the rule of God that she will take over the world and rule it before Jesus comes (Post-Millennialism). I believe that this view is wrong. Through the ministry of Jesus and the apostles, and through the Church today, the Kingdom of God has broken into this age. The Kingdom of God truly came in

Jesus. However, it came partially. The Kingdom is already here in one sense, yet not here in others. This "already but not yet" dynamic will typify this age until the return of Jesus. Whenever we see a body healed or a marriage restored by the power of God, there is the Kingdom. However, the full coming of the Kingdom rule over all the earth, as was the hope of the prophets, awaits the return of Jesus. In the present time, we should occupy until He comes and affect every realm of human life. Jesus is Lord of all! This age is one of warfare between the Kingdom of God and the kingdom of darkness. During this age we see various manifestations of both kingdoms. A company of rulers is being called out from every nation to rule as the Bride of the Messiah in the Age to Come. This is the age of transition. The Book of Revelation shows the war between the kingdom of darkness and the Kingdom of God coming to its final climax, followed by the ultimate victory of the Kingdom of God. By our engaging in warfare and seeking to establish the Kingdom by God's Spirit to the fullest extent of our God-led means, we "hasten the day of His coming," as Peter taught. We are involved with Messiah Jesus in bringing this transitional age to its climactic end.

With these thoughts in mind, we now turn to the Book of Revelation itself.

As I prepared for Passover 1990, the Lord gave me a seven-point outline of the Book of Revelation. (see Table of Contents). The next seven chapters follow this outline. Further preparation for this book came through a study of the Book of Isaiah over a six-month period. I believe that the three most important sources for understanding the Book of Revelation are the Hebrew accounts of the Passover and Exodus and the texts concerning Israel's entrance into the promised land; the Book of Isaiah; and the Book of Daniel. Most of the themes of the Book of Revelation are anticipated in these writings. We will thus refer frequently to these materials. May you be blessed as you read this text along with the Book of Revelation. May you be prepared for spiritual warfare! Do Periodically review the **Table of Contents** to aid understanding.

Chapter I

PREPARATION OF GOD'S PEOPLE

Please read Revelation chapters one through four. (It is important that you read the Scripture texts before the material in each chapter of this book.)

John's Description of the Setting of His Revelation

The aged apostle John was exiled on the island of Patmos. The visions and words of the book we hold in our hands came to him in an extraordinary experience of rapture in the Holy Spirit. The natural mind cannot understand this. Those scholars who try to understand the Book of Revelation merely as a literary composition by an author using the literary devices and symbols common to his day completely miss the point. Of course the revelation given to John was presented in terms that could be understood by the first century reader. It was also given in terms that will be best understood by the people of God in the last days! However, our approach to the book is greatly lacking if we do not take John's testimony at face value. He was in the Spirit and had an experience with the Lord in which he was given the content of this prophecy. God Himself gave symbols and words that would speak to the understanding of the people of the day. In 1:3 we read, "Blessed is he who reads and those who hear the words of this prophecy, and keep those things which are written in it; for the time is near." We understand from these words that the people of God have been living in the last days since the outpouring of the Holy Spirit (Joel 2:28-32). The last of these last days will take place for the last generation of this transitional age, just prior to the return of the Messiah Jesus. However, it is God's intention that every generation be able to see themselves and their struggles in terms of this book.

The first century believers had a vivid sense that they could be the last generation of the age. In prophetic time, the events of the book were near. Many were those who lived through events like the ones typified in the Book of Revelation. Events matching the descriptions given in Revelation did happen: the persecution and scattering of Israel, the persecution of the saints, and the fall of "Babylon" and its religious system (the fall of Rome). Yet the events which fulfilled the prophecy of the book for the saints of early centuries in no way detracts from the fact that the fullest manifestations of its meaning will be for the generation alive at the coming of Jesus.

We see hereby the truth of the various interpretations explained in the Introduction. Believers encountering severe spiritual warfare are to see themselves in this book as perhaps the last generation before the return of the Lord. In prophetic time and application, "the time is near."

John addresses himself to the seven churches of Asia Minor. He encourages them by proclaiming the victory of Jesus the Messiah and our own place of rulership with Him as kings and priests to God. All the tribes of the earth will mourn and the nations will at last turn to the Lord at His coming (Zechariah 14, Isa. 45:22-25). The seven churches of Asia Minor (modern Turkey) were churches for which John was responsible as an apostle. The reader should note the importance of this. Interpreters have too easily identified the seven churches as seven progressive periods of Church history. In my view, all seven messages have great relevance to all churches of all ages. Dispensationalists of the nineteenth century saw themselves as the Philadelphian church, which alone was fully commended! The Church to come after them, which they already saw coming on the scene, was the Laodicean church, lukewarm and about to be spewed out of the mouth of the Lord. However, those who believe in the restoration of the Body of Believers to unity, power, love, holiness and glory before Jesus comes should see a problem in the Laodiceans representing the state of the Church just before the rapture.

In dispensational thought, the Church will not be here for the events of the Book of Revelation. This is not my view. The book was written to edify us for our spiritual warfare. It is true that we may see one or another of these churches as being more characteristic of a given period in Church history or of a church within a particular geographic location. Some have said the American church at the end of the twentieth century is

Laodicean. We certainly would not say this of the Church of the third world or of China! Indeed, many of the problems of the other churches in these chapters are also found in churches of every age. Therefore, although there may be great applications of these texts for churches today and great warnings for the Church of the last days, I believe that there is no warrant in the text for seeing the intended meaning as other than as simply stated, messages for the seven literal churches that existed in Asia Minor at the end of the first century.

In 1:12-13 John has a great vision of Jesus, "One like the Son of Man," in the midst of seven lampstands. The seven lampstands are the light of the Holy Spirit's power and testimony shining forth from the seven churches. Seven is the number of perfection. As we know from other texts (such as in Zechariah), the Holy Spirit is as the oil that gives the ability to lamps to burn. Jesus is the testimony of the churches; He is in the midst of the lampstands. Verse 20 makes the interpretation of the symbols clear:

> *"The mystery of the seven stars which you saw in My right hand, and the seven golden lampstands: The seven stars are the angels of the seven churches, and the seven lampstands which you saw are the seven churches."*

Some have interpreted the "seven angels" to be the head pastors of each church. "Angel" can also be interpreted as "messenger." (This is the basis of the Baptist tradition of calling pastoral delegates to governing conventions "messengers.") Since John writes to the angel of each church, it is probable that he is not speaking of a guardian angel of the church, but a human leader who can receive the word. It is possible that these churches were of such a size that the leaders were not local pastors as we understand the term, but overseers of several congregations.

The Letters to the Seven Churches

The seven letters precede the prophecies of what is yet to come because the Church must be zealous and holy to face the spiritual warfare of the last days. Only then will victory be assured. Those who are not holy and full of God will succumb to the enemy. Therefore these letters are a preparation for the people of God. All seven letters have tremendous implications for God's people in the last days. If the Body of the Messiah can heed the warnings of these letters and be restored, we will become the glorious Bride without spot or wrinkle and will enter into the victory of the Lord.

The first church addressed in 2:1-7 is *the church of Ephesus*. Although commended for testing apostles, for showing patience and perseverance, and for laboring for the Lord, the church is severely warned for having left their first love. They are called upon to repent so as not to lose their lampstand (the light and power of witness through the presence of the Spirit). Again and again the word comes: **"Hear what the Spirit says to the churches...to him who overcomes,"** Jesus will give great rewards. These rewards are variously described in the letters to the churches. Here the description is of eating from the tree of life in the paradise of God. The Church is also commended for rejecting the Nicolaitans, which some believe combined gnostic heresies with their biblical faith.

I believe it is most important to realize that the primary faith challenge of the believer and the corporate Body is to maintain a fervent heart of love for the Lord. All acceptable works flow from this love, which is crucial preparation for the battle to come and for every battle and trial in life. This alone will enable us to maintain right motives. We are to stir ourselves up to this love by meditating on what the Lord has done for us and has promised us. We are to stir ourselves to be filled with the Holy Spirit (Eph. 5:18) as a key way to maintain this love. Psalms, hymns and spiritual songs are means of God to maintain a Spirit-filled life. God commanded the sons of Israel to love Him with all their heart, soul and strength (Deut. 6:5); the New Covenant promises the ability to fulfill the command. Radical love for God and His Son is the key preparation for the last days.

Revelation 2:8-11 describes a church that has been persecuted. Some of this has come from Jewish impostors (those not born Jewish, but taking on Jewish practices and persecuting the believers who did not, or those from the Jewish leadership who pressured the believers with false doctrine, accusation and attempts to woo believers away from the truth). Their tribulation will last ten days (a number symbolizing completion). The call is to be fearless. Fearlessness is a product of fervent love and faith in God which is fully present even in the midst of severe trial. This is a major step of preparation for all believers in the end times. Such faith is built by a devotional life that includes the discipline of meditating on the Lord's promises and seeing them established in our lives as reflections of God's own character. The reward for faithfulness even unto death is the crown of life (resurrection and rulership with Jesus).

We are told that overcomers will not be hurt by the second death. Indeed, this death, described in Revelation 20, is a final separation from God. John does not contemplate salvation for people who only give lip service to the Kingdom of God! *The Pergamos church* has also experienced persecution. Satan has a throne in Pergamos, which could be the false religious system of the empire expressed there or other false cults. The Pergamos believers did not deny Jesus even when they lost a faithful martyr, Antipas. The word "martyr" means *witness*. The early Church understood that the highest witness was testimony given in the face of death.

Despite these reasons for commendation, the church at Pergamos is rebuked for holding the doctrine of Balaam, who sought money for his prophetic ability. He also led Israel to commit sexual immorality so that she would lose her favor with God, and the pagan King Balak could defeat her. Again we read of the Nicolaitans. Did these Nicolaitans teach a sexual liberty (like the later libertarian gnostics) as part of grace? They would thus be tools of Satan to spiritually weaken the believers that he might defeat them. They are called upon to repent or be subject to the severe judgment of the Lord.

It is obvious from this passage that the godly congregation must enforce its standards of discipline for violations of basic biblical doctrine and morality. Overcomers in this congregation are promised hidden manna (the treasures of the Word of God) and a white stone with a new name written on it. The latter typifies a gem reflecting our new name, which refers to our distinctive character and calling in the Kingdom of God.

The church at Thyatira is also commended for faith, patience and works (v. 19). However, a woman named Jezebel is tolerated. She is a false prophetess who beguiles servants of God to commit sexual immorality and to eat what is sacrificed to idols. She was given time to repent, but now severe judgment is decreed upon her and upon those who commit adultery with her.

Apparently Jezebel beguiled the church into secret doctrines called "the depths of Satan" (v. 24). Again, this has gnostic overtones. (Gnostics were heretics who taught secret knowledge and mysteries as the means of salvation.) Some have noted that the characteristics of Jezebel in this chapter are amazingly similar to those of Queen Jezebel of Israel and her role during the days of King Ahab. This has given rise to a teaching in the Charismatic church concerning a principality of Jezebel which establishes destructive, manipulative patterns in the Church among those people who yield to it. Perhaps even in this section of Revelation, Jezebel is not the literal name of the woman involved, but is used as a name for her and others of similar ilk because they are characterized by the same sins as the queen of old.

There is a Jezebelian work of Satan in the Church which is characterized by manipulative prophecy, a prophetic putting forth of strange doctrine and the domination of weak men for Satan's advantage. This is especially true in those congregations in which there is no strong governing male eldership. Amazingly, this condition produces spiritual impotence in the men of a congregation and a diminishing of the real gifts of the Spirit among the people. As Elijah was demoralized by Queen Jezebel, so men sometimes feel powerless before this Jezebel spirit. This situation sometimes leads to actual sexual immorality. I have seen this problem many times in various churches throughout my last twenty years of ministry.

The Thyatirans are promised a part in ruling the nations if they overcome. The fact that Psalm 2:8-9 is quoted is significant in this regard. The psalm promises the Messiah rulership over the nations. So the manchild of Revelation 12, a reference primarily to the Messiah, is described as ruling the nations with a rod of iron. This strong rulership is here applied to the Bride of the Messiah. His rulership is also our rulership. We are destined to rule with Him. Therefore the psalm is interpreted as applying to all who overcome. Actually, all the promises to overcomers in these seven letters apply to all overcoming believers. That we are given the morning star means we will participate in the revelation of His coming, which is also our full manifestation as the sons of God (Rom. 8:19). Indeed, when He appears we shall see the dawn of the Millennium for all the earth.

In 3:1-6 we read of the *Sardis church*. This is a group having significant activity, but the activity is primarily dead works. Since only works that proceed from a heart of love for the Lord are perfect, the believers at Sardis are called upon to repent. The warnings are severe, even to the point of calling into question the salvation of those who do not overcome. The Lord will come as a thief to those who perform mere good works of the flesh, but do not truly know and walk with Him. These works are defiling. First Thessalonians chapter five makes it clear that those who are not in darkness will find that the coming of the Lord does not overtake them as a thief. The promise for those who are worthy is to wear the white garments of purity and priesthood, having their names inscribed in the Book of Life.

In 3:7-13 we read of the *Philadelphian church*. This congregation is praised above all. The Messiah, Jesus, has the key of David and is in control of opening and closing opportunities for His people. This Church is also under persecution from the synagogue of Satan (either false converts to Judaism or groups of Jews who were perverting gospel teaching). Those of that "synagogue" will bow before the Philadelphians. These believers will be kept from the hour of trial which will come upon all the earth. Nineteenth century Dispensationalists viewed themselves as the Philadelphians within their scheme of interpreting the seven letters as seven successive periods of Church history. The Laodicean Age was beginning, they taught, and they saw themselves in an overlapping period. Hence they viewed the concept of being kept from the hour of trial as a promise that the true Church would be raptured into heaven before the seven-year tribulation began. The Bride of the Messiah would be absent from the great tribulation.

I believe this dispensational teaching is wrong and impractical. The promise for the Philadelphians is meant for all true believers for the trials, the plagues and the other judgments which follow in the Book of Revelation. However, this does not mean the Church will be raptured out of the earth. As we shall show, the foreshadowing events of the Book of Revelation are found in the Passover of Exodus. Israel was kept from the hour of trial (the plagues of judgment upon Egypt) by being protected in the land of Goshen. We see in the Book of Revelation that God will have His Goshens for His people, keeping them from the hour of trial. This does not mean that some will not be called to sanctify the Name of God as martyr witnesses. However, Jesus promised that not a hair of our heads would be lost, even though some would be sent to death. This is how complete the promise of the resurrection is. Some are kept from the trial by being able to sing through the flames, as did Ridley and Latimer in 17th century England. Others will be kept in supernatural protection in cities of refuge that will be like Goshen. No matter what God's manner of keeping us safe, we will not be subject to His judgments and will only be subject to the call and will of the Spirit of God concerning our witness in the last days. For some this will mean supernatural escape from the forces of evil. For others it will mean enduring these forces even unto death by supernatural enabling.

Overcomers will be pillars in God's Temple, marked by the Name of God and part of the everlasting New Jerusalem (Rev. 21:9-21). We will be given our new name, showing forth our eternal calling and nature in the Messiah.

Revelation 3:13-22 describes the lukewarm *Laodicean Church*. God hates lukewarmness and will spew out those who are of this heart. A lack of perception of their true condition causes the Laodiceans to see themselves as spiritually strong and wealthy. This wealth need not necessarily include great material riches, but could include financial means. Yet God proclaims the true condition of this church: "Wretched, miserable, poor, blind and naked." The healing of this condition is described as requiring the buying of gold refined in the fire, white garments for clothing and salve to restore sight. This includes the act of repentance, covering sin by the blood of the Lamb and the rekindling of the fire of love for the Father, the Lord Jesus and the Holy Spirit. Only when this love burns within are we clothed. Only then is our spiritual perception solid. God rebukes those He loves. He chastens only His children. This is the message of the Book of Hebrews concerning chastening (Heb. 12:5-11).

The great invitation to rekindle fellowship with the Lord is extended in verse 20. A feast of fellowship is the reward of fully opening the door to the Lord. The opening of the door is the offering to Him of the whole of our lives, keeping nothing back. It is noteworthy that the overcomers are herein promised a place of sitting with the Lord on His throne. Ephesians 2:6 describes the life of the Spirit-filled believer as seated with Him now in the heavenlies. This promise for the overcomer completes the picture of Ephesians and is similar to the promise of Revelation 2:26-27.

John Is Called to Heaven

Chapter four begins with John being called into Heaven. Some have also seen this as a reference to the rapture of the saints before the great tribulation. This is improbable. Rather, John is called up to see the rest of the vision. This is a visionary calling up, not a prophecy of a future event.

The visions of the rest of the Revelation certainly provide literal meanings for those who are conversant with the symbolism of the Hebrew Scriptures and the first century setting of the book. However, it is difficult to know where symbolism and literal meaning can be fully distinguished. John is telling us what he saw. Is this the way these realities forever appear in Heaven? Or is this the way God gives the visionary experience for the best understanding of realities that go beyond what can be literally put forth? Are there really creatures that look like the ones described as full of literal eyes (v. 6), or is this a symbol of a spiritual reality? The vision is reality; but exactly what kind of reality it might be is beyond the grasp of our limited human minds.

In the visions to come, the veil between Heaven and earth is opened. John sees into the unseen world which has such a great effect on our seen world (even as our world affects that realm). John is called to Heaven and told that he will see the things which will come to pass. He was immediately in the Spirit and beheld a throne! When God grants such an experience, the person is not conscious of his physical, earthly being. As Paul stated, he did not know whether he was in his body or out of it when he was caught up to Heaven (II Cor. 12:2-4). It does not matter, for in such experiences the meaning of spacial location and bodily limitation is transcended.

In the opening verses of chapter four, we read of John's extraordinary experience of God as jasper and sardius stone in appearance. An emerald rainbow is over the throne, around which are twenty-four thrones. Twenty-four elders clothed in white robes with crowns of gold on their heads sit on these thrones. The possibilities of interpretation of these twenty-four elders are many and not necessarily exclusive. The number twenty-four is a multiple of twelve. There are twelve tribes of Israel and twelve original apostles, corresponding to the names on the gates and the foundation stones of the New Jerusalem (Rev. 21). Are these twenty-four the corporate representation of the Old and New Testament saints before the throne of God? Is it possible that the elders are a vision of the actual presence of the twelve patriarchs and the twelve apostles before the throne? Both of these are possibilities. The twenty-four corporately represent the continual praise of all God's people before the throne of grace. However, this does not exclude the spiritual presence of each individual believer as seated with Christ in heavenly places (Eph. 2:6). The white robes are the garb of priestly service and purity. The crowns represent the reward of eternal fruit and the authority of rule.

The descriptions of the sea of glass, the seven lamps burning as the perfection of God's Spirit and the four living creatures are a picture of awesome majesty. God's Spirit is not divided into seven, but seven represents the perfection of the presence of the Spirit. The qualities of the living creatures around the throne represent the majesty and rule of the lion, the intelligence and quality of man in the image of God, the swiftness of the eagle and the steadiness of the calf. The many eyes represent fulness of vision. Four may be the picture of universality in rule, four being the number of directions, north, south, east and west. The picture of continual rapturous worship is more than we can comprehend. The living creatures cry out "Holy, holy, holy," and the twenty-four elders fall down before Him, casting their crowns in submission, for their rulership is fully under the Father. The hymn of praise is glorious.

> *"You are worthy, O Lord, to receive glory and honor and power; for You created all things, and by Your will they exist and were created" (v.11).*

We learn in chapter five that the figure represented upon the throne is none other than the Father, for the Son will take a scroll from Him. This is reminiscent of the picture of the Son receiving rulership from the Ancient of Days in Daniel chapter seven. The Lamb's taking of the scroll begins the Scriptures concerning the judgments of God. The parallels to Passover-Exodus now begin in a wonderful way.

CHAPTER TWO

THE PLAGUES OF GOD ON WORLDWIDE EGYPT

The Passover-Exodus Key

It is the Lamb of God who will open the seals that will begin the worldwide judgments and events of God's visitation upon the earth in the last days, even the Day of the Lord. At this point it is well to summarize the order of the parallels found throughout the book. This will enable the reader to follow the power of this interpretation.

The Passover-Exodus account describes the people of God as being engaged in a severe struggle with Egypt and her ruler, Pharaoh. For the sake of Israel and of His own purposes in the earth, God raised up two prophets, Moses and Aaron, who announced plagues upon Egypt. The first nine plagues did not result in repentance on the part of the Egyptians or their leader. During these plagues, the children of Israel were protected in the land of Goshen. God made a distinction between the Egyptians and the children of Israel in this way. This was an unmistakably supernatural sign. However, the tenth plague, the death of the firstborn throughout the land of Egypt, resulted in Pharaoh's releasing the children of Israel. The number ten is significant, since in Hebrew thought it is the number of completion. Ten plagues represent complete judgment upon Egypt.

After the Israelites left their places of abode, Pharaoh's heart was once again hardened. He pursued the Israelites to the edge of the sea. Israel was hemmed in by water on one side and the soldiers of Egypt on the other. Although they were protected from the forces of Egypt by the pillars of fire and cloud, there appeared to be no way of escape. It was then that God told Moses to go forward. When he stretched his rod over the sea, it was divided and the Israelites passed through to the other side upon dry ground. The amazingly foolish Egyptians pursued Israel into the sea. At God's command, the waters came together and the army of Pharaoh was drowned. The astonished people of Israel found themselves on the other side. Israel was free; she could now receive the Covenant of God and enter the land of promise. It should be noted as well that Israel was protected from the most severe plague, the death of the firstborn, by placing the blood of the Passover lamb upon the entryways to their dwellings.

The parallels to this in the Book of Revelation are truly amazing. We shall bring these out in detail in the following chapters. This truth has great implications for how we see and pass through the trials and battles soon to be upon the people of God.

> *The world parallels the Egypt of Exodus. The people of God are represented by the Israelites in Egypt. As Israel was protected in Goshen, so God will mark believers and protect them from the plagues. Unlike the Israelites, the believers will be protected in various places throughout the world. The sons of Israel overcame the angel of death because the blood of the lamb was upon their doorposts. Believers in the last days will overcome Satan by the blood of the Lamb (Jesus), by the word of their testimony and by not loving their own lives unto death. The Antichrist of the last days is parallelled by the Pharaoh. Furthermore, the last days people of God will have an extraordinary escape, as did the Israelites in their escape through the sea. This time, the believers are taken through the veil between the seen and unseen worlds into Heaven and return with the Messiah. As the Egyptians foolishly pursued Israel, so the armies of the Antimessiah will foolishly pursue Israel by sending his armies into her land to oppose the nation of the Jews and the armies of Heaven returning with the Messiah. As Pharaoh's troops were supernaturally defeated in the sea, so the armies of the Antichrist will be supernaturally defeated in a great conflagration* (Revelation 19, Zechariah 14).

There were ten plagues upon Egypt. Even so, there are twenty-one segments of revelation and judgment revealed in the Book of Revelation. This includes seven seals, seven trumpets and seven bowls of God's wrath.

Twenty-one is the product of three times seven; seven is
the number of perfection and three, the number of God.
Hence twenty-one represents God's perfection of judgment. Ten represents complete judgment. It is significant that several plagues are similar in type to the
plagues upon Egypt. *However, everything that happens
paralleling the plagues upon Egypt is now intensified, both in
scope and in devastating results.* As Pharaoh and the Egyptians hardened their hearts despite the plagues, so most
of the peoples of the world will harden their hearts
toward God. Because of this, the escape of the believers
is more extraordinary than the escape through the sea.

The Book of Revelation brings a finality of judgment
that was only proximate in the Exodus. Israel experienced protection from the plagues in Egypt, but ob-
served the drowning of the Egyptians from the other
side of the sea. So the true disciples of Jesus will experience deliverance from the plagues of the seven seals
and seven trumpets upon earth in our natural bodies,
but will execute the judgments of God in our coming
with Jesus from the other side. *The bowls of God's wrath
are poured out upon the world at the time of our coming with
Him to execute judgment upon the armies that have come up
to Jerusalem.* After that judgment, we enter the promised
land of millennial rule with the Messiah.

*Two prophets are mentioned as calling forth plagues upon
the earth in Revelation 11. These are parallels to Moses and
Aaron.* They may be literal persons, but I believe they
also represent prophetic ministry. I personally believe
the two witnesses are literal prophetic spokesman in the
last days. However, I believe there will be many
prophetic voices raised up to speak with power in all the
nations of the world.

It should also be noted that among the descriptions of the seven seals, trumpets and bowls of wrath, there are several *excurses* in the book. These chapters give a more detailed picture of some aspect of the last days situation of the people of God in their battle with the enemy. These excurses will be so noted.

The Lamb Who Is Worthy Takes the Scroll (5:1-14)

In 5:1 the Father is portrayed as holding a scroll in His hand. The scroll is sealed with seven seals. (Ancient scrolls were sealed in a manner similar to our sealing letters with sealing wax and stamping them with a symbol of the sender.) No one was found to open this scroll and John wept.

We are told that the Lion of the tribe of Judah, Jesus the Messiah, has prevailed to open the scroll. Here we see the vision of a Lamb as though it had been slain who takes the scroll from the hand of the Father (vs. 6-7). The nature of the symbolic portrayals in John's vision become clear in this instance. Jesus the Messiah is human and divine, but is not literally a lamb; nor did He take on the form of a lamb and so dwell among us. However, in symbol, we see the role of Jesus as the sacrificial Lamb. By His sacrifice and resurrection He has the right to take the scroll and open it. The scroll represents the decrees of God concerning the acts of judgment and redemption to occur in the last days. The seven seals represent the seven judgments. These are progressive. However, the seventh seal includes the judgments of the seven trumpets, and the seventh trumpet includes the judgments of the seven bowls of God's wrath. Thus there is a limited overlap. I believe that the seals opened by the Lamb show Him as having the authority to initiate all the judgments to follow.

In verse 8, the four living creatures and the twenty-four elders fall down and worship the Lamb. The divinity of Jesus, who is worthy to receive this level of worship, is well shown in this verse. As we noted before, the twenty-four elders represent the people of God. Therefore, they hold golden bowls of incense representing the prayers of all the saints. The harps may represent the worship of the saints. This representative role is well shown in their singing to the Lamb. Out of every tribe, tongue and nation we have been redeemed and have been made kings and priests to our God (Rev. 7:14-15.) We shall reign on earth.

The reader would do well to meditate on the great hymns found in this chapter. Ten thousand times ten thousand angels, as well as many others, join in the worship. After this, John hears all the creatures in the universe join in prayer. Revelation chapter five is one of the great inspirational chapters in the Bible. Its symbolism elicits a tremendous sense of holy wonder and awe.

The Seven Seals (6:1-17, 8:1-6)

To this point we have been following the order of the Book of Revelation. However, after our description of the seals, we will leave this progression to follow the topical outline suggested by the Passover-Exodus story. I believe this is warranted, that I might fully show the power of these parallels for understanding the book.

With the seals, we enter into the first plagues with parallels in the Exodus story. Not all the plagues of

Revelation are represented in the Exodus story; some are unique.

The first seal reveals a white horse and a rider with a bow and a crown. He is given the right to conquer. War is loosed upon the earth; this is a warfare that produces an increase of power for the conqueror which could be the conquering of world government. Throughout the rest of the Book of Revelation, we will see that events on earth are not to be understood in terms of natural causation. Rather, there are supernatural dimensions to the events on earth. This integral connection of the seen to the unseen world is far more extensive than we realize.

The second seal reveals a horseman on a fiery red horse. He is given authority to take peace from the earth. War is clearly intended; people will kill one another. This is the meaning of the great sword given him. This warfare is a more universal condition on earth.

The third seal reveals a black horse with a rider holding scales. The scales represent buying and selling agricultural commodities. The price of the goods represents the beginnings of scarcity upon the earth.

The fourth seal reveals a pale horse with a rider called Death. Hades (the grave) followed him. He is given power over a fourth of the earth to kill with sword (war), hunger (famine), death and by the beasts of the earth. It is not difficult to see the involvement of principalities and powers and spiritual warfare in the great famines and shortages in Africa, Russia and Central America. Devastating wars are one of the great reasons for some of these disasters, as in Ethiopia. Although it is not clearly spelled out, the plagues upon Egypt destroyed crops and livestock, producing famine, scarcity and death.

This weakened Egypt for years and caused her not to be a factor when Israel conquered the land of Canaan.

The fifth seal reveals the martyrs. The judgment shown in the vision of the martyrs is vengeance for their blood which will be exacted from those who dwell upon the earth.

There are important implications in these verses. First, the time of vengeance will occur when the number of the martyrs' fellow servants is complete. Paul teaches that we fill up that which is lacking in the sufferings of the Messiah. The Messiah fully paid the price for our sins. However, our witness to His death and resurrection requires all to suffer, some even unto death. This suffering fulfills our witnessing responsibility to the Kingdom of God. When this suffering is complete, the fulness of God's judgment and redemption will be poured out.

The witness of believers will lead some to repentance and salvation. It will lead to the hardening of some hearts and to severe judgment. The blood of the martyrs releases God's power in both mercy and judgment, depending upon human response. The vengeance of God will come soon. The priestly role of the saintly martyrs is portrayed by their priestly robes. The full number of martyrs is one which includes all the martyrs from Stephen until the rapture of the saints. The rapture takes place upon the completing of the number of martyrs.

Before the rapture, several other completions take place. First, the gospel of the Kingdom will be preached in all the world as a witness (Matt. 24:12-14), and a full company from all nations will make up the Bride of the Messiah. I believe that, in spite of the hardening of the hearts of the majority of the peoples of the world, *the Church will see its greatest harvest from all the world's peoples*

during the last days. This is the "fulness of the Gentiles"
(Rom. 11:25). There will be a full revelation of evil in the
Antichrist, his false occult religious system and
economic tyranny (II Thessalonians 2). The Bride of the
Messiah will come to maturity, or completeness, in unity,
love and power before she will be with Him where He is
(John 17:24). This will be the time of her most powerful
witness. It is the restoration of the people of God before
the Messiah comes. *Lastly, Israel's leaders will call upon
Jesus to save them in their final great war* with the words,
"Blessed is He who comes in the name of the Lord"
(Matt. 23:39).

The sixth seal reveals a great earthquake, the sun becoming dark, the moon becoming as blood, the stars of
the heavens dropping, the sky rolled up as a scroll and
the mountains and islands being moved out of their
places. So great is this cataclysmic judgment that all
types of people hide in caves and in the rocks of the
mountains, saying,

> *"Fall on us and hide us from the face of Him who sits
> on the throne and from the wrath of the Lamb! For
> the great day of His wrath has come, and who is able
> to stand?" (vs. 16-17)*

Compare this passage with Joel 2:28-32. After the
Spirit is poured out, we read of the sun being darkened
and the moon turning to blood before the great day of
God's wrath and vengeance. Joel has many references to
the events of the Book of Revelation, even to the final
war in the land of Israel described in Revelation 19 and
Joel 3. Partial fulfillments of this prophecy were seen
when Jesus died on the cross: The sun became dark and

a great earthquake occurred. (Was this a factor in the rending of the veil in the Temple?) However, the ultimate fulfillment of Joel's words concerning the fulness of the outpouring of the Holy Spirit in a latter rain and the awesome judgment of God still awaits an ultimate and final fulfillment.

It is well to note that the people described in the sixth seal are not repentant or calling upon God for salvation. Again, the place where symbolic and literal description divides is difficult to discern. Earth and Heaven still exist after the sixth seal. The sun may turn dark in eclipses. Volcanic eruptions and earthquakes can darken the sun and make the moon appear to be red. Stars falling could refer to rulers and heavenly principalities. However, the description of the heavens rolling up as a scroll seems to be a symbolic description of heavens that disappear to human sight because of these awful judgments. Recall that the darkening of the sun was one of the judgments upon Egypt.

Revelation six ends with the proclamation that the day of God's wrath has come. This would be seen in light of the fact that the seventh seal is ready to be taken from the scroll. This seal includes the seven trumpets, and the seven bowls of God's wrath, which are within the seventh trumpet. The specific succession of events follows these symbols of seals, trumpet and bowls.

We begin to clearly see that plagues are now to be poured out upon a world that is to the people of God as Egypt was to the children of Israel. (We will skip chapter seven at this time; it topically fits our next chapter.)

In 8:1-6, we read of *the seventh seal*. This seal reveals the seven angels with seven trumpets (which could be *shoferot*, or rams' horns). An angel with a golden censer offers incense with the prayers of the saints upon the golden altar. These prayers ascend before God. Apparently the prayers of the saints are affecting events in Heaven and on earth. Intercession brings God's mighty judgments and redemptive acts. Hence, when the censer is thrown to earth there are "noises, thundering, lightnings, and an earthquake."

The First Six Trumpets (8:1-9:21)

The first trumpet produced hail and fire mingled with blood. This plague burned up a third of the trees and all green grass.

When the *second angel sounded his trumpet*, something like a burning mountain was thrown into the sea and a third of the sea became blood. One third of the living creatures in the sea died and a third of the ships were destroyed. We can see parallels here to the hail in the Exodus plagues and the water turning to blood.

The third trumpet reveals a great star which falls from heaven, burning like a torch. Once again, these events could be literal, as in the falling to earth of large meteors (trumpets two and three). They could also be means of describing what is unseen but has effects on the seen world. We do not know where to draw the lines. The plague of this trumpet produces bitter waters which cause death. We can see a limited fulfillment of this in our water pollution problems, which produce death rapidly in some third world environments or lead to disease and gradual decline in health in many more advanced parts of the world.

The fourth trumpet darkens a third of the light of the moon, stars and sun. As with the sixth seal, this could

literally be the effect of earthquakes and volcanic eruptions, nuclear wars, or a combination of the two. The
fourth trumpet also depicts an angel who cries three
woes because of the next three trumpets.

The fifth trumpet releases the locusts from the bottomless pit. The sun and air were darkened, both from the
number of locusts and from the smoke from the pit. The
locusts are described as having scorpion-like power.
They are only to harm those men who do not have the
seal of God on their heads. Here we note that *God distin-
guishes the people of God from the people of the world.* Just as
the Israelites in Egypt, the people of God are not subject
to the plagues. (We will describe the people of God and
their protection in depth in the following chapter.)

The locusts are given authority to torment men for
five months with a torment like a scorpion sting. The
description of the locusts—shaped like horses, heads
with crowns of gold and faces like men—tells us that this
is more than an insect plague made up of a strange type
of stinging locust. There may be a literal locust plague
during this time. However, since the Book of Revelation
tears away the veil between the seen and unseen worlds,
we could see the locusts as demonic hosts released to torment men. Human beings bring demonic attack upon
themselves. This attack is ultimately under the control of
God. Men hate the attack, but at the same time invite it
by their evil behavior. Demons aspire to torment people
because they hate man, who is created in God's image.
God is able to use the demonic hosts, which are under
His judgment, as instruments of judgment in the world.

The amazing description continues in verses 8-10 of
chapter nine. It is best to simply let this description

speak for itself. The king of the locusts is the angel of the bottomless pit, Abaddon, the destroyer.

The parallel to the Exodus is clear in the plague of locusts. However, this plague is worldwide and on a much different plane than one of ordinary locusts. It is the Exodus plague intensified. In verse 6, we read that men will seek death and not find it. They are afraid to live and afraid to die. Yet, as the Egyptians, they do not repent and turn to the living God.

The sixth trumpet sounds and John hears a voice from the golden altar saying, "Release the four angels who are bound at the great river Euphrates" (v. 14). These angels are released to kill a third of mankind.

Throughout the Book of Revelation, we find parallels to the Book of Hebrews. In the latter book we read that the Tabernacle of old is symbolic of spiritual realities in Heaven, the heavenly Tabernacle. In Revelation we read of the altar, the censer, the golden altar and other pictures of the reality of God and His place of abode.

With *the sixth trumpet* (9:13-21), we read of an incredible army on horses. The riders have breastplates of fiery red, blue and yellow. The horses have heads of lions and breathe fire and smoke. They do harm with their mouths and tails. Some have seen this as describing awesome demonic powers which seek to destroy mankind. Yet they are under God's control and limitations. He uses their desire to destroy as part of His bringing judgment on mankind. Others have seen this as a reference to huge armies, such as China's military. They come from beyond the Euphrates (the east). Modern military vehicles and tanks could appear like this in a vision, especially to one of John's time. Modern artillery "stings" from the head and the tail. It is well to leave the full meaning of the identification to God. The description goes beyond what can be identified in human terms. Aspects of military power may be bound together with the supernatural agency of demonic powers. The number of people killed would be over a billion and a half today.

Amazingly, those not killed by the plagues did not repent of their works,

> *"that they should not worship demons, and idols of gold, silver, brass, stone, and wood, which can neither see nor hear nor walk; and they did not repent of their murders or their sorceries or their sexual immoralities or their thefts" (vs. 20-21).*

In our present experience we see that God's judgments produce anger among many, but not repentance. People debate the problem of evil and ask how a good God could allow such evil to fall upon mankind. Yet we must see that we are not in the full favor of God's protection. We are a world under judgment for our sin. God does not see us as the "good guys" that we perceive ourselves to be. Such judgments should bring humanity to repentance. The plagues are a result of our sin. As we look at plagues and disasters throughout history, and especially today, we see that they do not usually bring men to repent before a Holy God. The AIDS plague, other venereal diseases, famines and disasters are the result of gross sin, greed, shortsightedness and hatred in the human race. Yet God is blamed for the judgments which humanity brings upon itself. Surely the picture of these verses (20-21) is even now accurate.

The Mighty Angel and the Little Book (10:1-11)

The angel of the Book of Revelation is variously interpreted. For our purposes, an exact identification is unnecessary. Some have seen the figure as the Messiah because the description of majesty is so great. When he speaks, the voice of seven thunders sounds. (Seven, again, is the number of perfection.) The rainbow is a covenant sign, and the fact that he is "clothed with a [glory] cloud" surely reminds us of the revelation of God in the pillar of cloud to Moses and the children of Israel. Thunder is a description of the voice of God; the roar of a lion connotes kingship. In Psalm 29, we read that the voice of the Lord is powerful upon many waters. The person of Revelation 10 stands with a foot on the land and a foot on the sea. This implies authority or power over all the earth. Of course, the identification with the Messiah is not absolutely certain. Other passages in the Book of Revelation identify the Messiah outright.

Most significant to our purpose is verse 7, that tells us that in the days by the sounding of the seventh angel of the seventh shofar (trumpet), **"The mystery of God would be finished, as He declared to His servants the prophets."** What is this mystery? I believe it is none other than the completion of the Bride of the Messiah. In Pauline writings we read of the mystery of the Church revealed. "Mystery" in New Testament writings usually describes that which was previously hidden but is now revealed. This mystery is that Jew and Gentile are to be one Body in the Messiah *before the actual and full establishment of the worldwide Kingdom of the Messiah*. The Jewish people in the first century looked for a specific order of end-time events. The apostles shared much of this perspective. It is my view that before Acts 9, the Apostles believed in this order: First Israel would repent and turn to the Messiah, then He would deliver Israel from all her enemies. Only after this would the world see the truth and come to the knowledge of God. Then all the world would be one in faith as Zechariah 14:9 proclaims and all the prophets predicted.

Paul's great revelation in the Spirit was that God was, during his time, taking out of every nation a representative people who would constitute His ruling Bride. They would be His resurrected rulers of the age to come. The Bride foreshadows the age to come, in which Israel and the nations will be one under the rule of Jesus. To complete this mystery, I believe, implies both that the full representation from every nation has entered the Kingdom, and that the people of God have come into unity, power and holiness. This is the implication of the prayer of Jesus for the unity of His people in John 17. Paul also teaches this in Ephesians 4, wherein he says that the five-fold ministry will equip the saints until they come to the full stature of the maturity of the Messiah.

This verse is a clear indication that the Body of the Messiah is on earth during the days of the great tribulation until the seventh trumpet. As we shall see, this verse hints at the rapture of the saints.

John is told to eat the little book which is in the hand of the angel. It is sweet in his mouth but bitter in his stomach. The conclusion of the passage (v. 11) says that John will prophesy about many peoples, nations, tongues and kings. To be a channel of God's word is indeed sweet, but the messages of judgment are hard for the prophet to receive and deliver.

As we noted earlier, the progression of events in the Book of Revelation is best followed by studying the succession of the seals, trumpets and bowls. However, between the depictions of these judgments are passages containing more detailed descriptions of the events of the last days that do not constitute part of the progression. Rather, they give insight into the nature of the whole period or expand on one aspect of it. Such is the case with Revelation chapters 10, 11 and 12. (Most of Revelation 12 will be discussed in the following chapter.)

The Two Witnesses of Revelation 11

This chapter begins with the commandment to John to measure the Temple. The court is to be left out, for it is given to the Gentiles (nations). We are told that they will tread the holy city under foot for 42 months. The language here parallels Luke 21, where we are told that Jerusalem will be trodden down by the Gentiles until their time is complete. Is this the final act and manifestation of the trodding down? Or is this a reinstatement of Gentile control after it had been lifted? Many students of prophecy believe that Luke 21 was fulfilled when Jerusalem was captured in 1967. However, Israel has left the Temple Mount in Arab control for political and religious reasons. Some would see here a reference to pagan infiltration into the Church. However, I believe this is a reference to Israel's national struggles in the last days.

The description of the two witnesses which follows is most important. They prophesy for 1,260 days. This is the same as three and one half years on the lunar 360-day year. We learn that these witnesses have the power to "shut Heaven," that is, to speak drought into existence. They can also turn water into blood and strike the earth with all kinds of plagues as often as they desire.

The work of the two witnesses parallels the work of Aaron and Moses. Furthermore, Revelation 11 shows us that the plagues of the Book of Revelation do not simply happen as mysteries to mankind. Rather, they occur as a result of prophetic speaking. The world will have prophecy and warning before the great plagues occur through the prophetic word. This is a great key to the nature of the period of the Book of Revelation.

Just who are the two witnesses? Some have theorized that they are Enoch and Elijah come back to earth, since they never physically died; but following their return, the two prophets will die. (I would ask why they have to die, since believers who are alive at the time of the coming of Jesus will never experience the usual pattern of death.) This is one possiblility. Others have thought these will be two leading prophets of the last days, one representing the Jews, the other, the Gentiles. Some have thought that the two represent the ministries of the prophet and the apostle, which God is restoring in these last days. The two witnesses could either be a literal leading apostle and a prophet or they could simply be symbolic of the restoration of these ministries.

I believe God's people in the last days will see the restoration of apostles and prophets. This will include giftings of great authority and empowerment for ministry. This is a clear implication of Ephesians 4:11-16 and of the prayer of Jesus found in John 17. The conditions of the last days are very similar to those of the time of the Roman Empire. There is a world opposition to the Gospel, the Jewish people again are in their land and there is great warfare between the Church and the forces of darkness.

Some believe John's measuring the Temple implies the existence of a literal Temple during this time and would see a parallel in Second Thessalonians 2, where we read that the Antimessiah shall sit in the Temple of God and blaspheme. Yet, since the Body of Believers is also called the Temple of God, we are wise to wait until prophetic fulfillments make this clear. Our concern with the Book of Revelation should be less for speculation and more for our own preparation and understanding of present warfare. Measuring the Temple could be related to examining the people of God or to the area of the Holy City which is in view.

In light of our practical orientation, Revelation 11 indicates at least that there will be a restoration of prophetic ministry similar to the period of the first century and the writing of the Old Testament. Personally, I believe there will be many prophets in the Body of the Messiah. They will give guidance to the last days Church for waging spiritual war. They will also announce judgments to the nations. We are seeing the restoration of prophets today. This restoration has not yet come to the point of power and prominence described in Revelation 11.

The 1989 San Francisco earthquake is a case in point. There were prophets of God who predicted the quake. It occurred on the first day of baseball's World Series while the nation looked on via television. Before the first pitch was thrown, the quake struck. Although there was some loss of life, the quake was not of major proportions. Prophets of stature and credibility have not yet become known to the public; thus there was no recognized voice

announcing the coming judgment and no later interpretation of it to the public. Yet when the last days
plagues and judgments occur; public prediction will precede the judgments. People will have ample evidence
from which to perceive that the events are judgments
from God. They will be fully responsible to repent.

This will be reminiscent of the situation in ancient
Egypt when Moses and Aaron announced the plagues
and judgments upon the Egyptians. However, these
judgments will be intensified in severity and in
worldwide scope. I believe the two witnesses represent
the most prominent of the last days prophets. The two
have world renown. Will the two prophets be literal
figures in Jerusalem? Will they be a Jew and a Gentile?
Will they be representatives of the restoration of the
apostles and prophets in the last days? All of these are
good possibilities. I personally believe there will be two
literal prophets in Jerusalem in the last days. However, I
also believe that the two prophets represent the
prophetic gifting being restored all over the world.
Kings and presidents will be called to take heed. They
will tremble at the words of God's last days' prophets.
However, as we see here, this does not mean they will
repent.

The guidance of the Body of believers is also important. The worldwide Church in the last days will be following apostles and prophets. We will be told to leave
cities before bombs drop, earthquakes hit or plagues are
poured out. Through prophetic guidance we will be
protected. Some reject this thought, since all believers
have the Spirit and can receive guidance from God. I
believe that because all true believers have the Holy
Spirit dwelling within, the inner witness of confirmation

is very important. *Those with pure and humble hearts will confirm the guidance from God's true prophets.* However, those who reject this ministry because they also have the Spirit are too individualistic. We are a corporate body. There will be corporate leading for congregations. God will speak to His corporate Body through His captains, to churches of the city and for the Church worldwide. Each individual will not receive the revelation for the Body, but he will receive it through leadership. If we are proud and do not realize that corporate leading will come from apostles and prophets, we will be in danger for our lives. Such will be the conditions of the last days.

We will have to learn to move as God's spiritual army, in discipline and in ranks. Confirmation will be important; but so will knowing who is trustworthy and can be followed. We will not always have days in which to decide whether or not we confirm each word as from the Lord. Our hearts need to be so sharp that we will immediately bear witness or not to the leading of God's apostles and prophets. We will know those called to lead us through the battles. However, only the humble and pure in heart will have the ability to follow and confirm rightly. This will be part of the way Jesus will purify His Church. The proud and individualistic will be cut off.

The key preparations for the last days are therefore holiness of heart, humility, a burning love for the Lord and a faith preparation through the Word that will enable us to find God's guidance and strength to withstand the onslaught of the enemy.

God's holy people can be martyred only when He calls upon them to lay down their lives. When we are free of sin, we have His great protection, even through the times of the Book of Revelation. The prophets are supernaturally protected from all who desire to harm them.

Fire proceeds from their mouths and devours their enemies. I believe this means the words from God that proceed from their mouths produce fiery judgments.

The prophets are finally overcome by the beast from the pit (Satan) and killed. The hearts of the people of the world are then revealed, for they rejoice and give gifts to one another. Instead of repenting, they are glad that the ones they blamed for the plagues are dead. For three and a half days their dead bodies lie in the city, spiritually called Sodom and Egypt, where our Lord was crucified. This could be a reference to last days Jerusalem. Until the Jewish leadership turns to Jesus they will make compromises with the Antimessiah even against believers. Yet the last acts of the Antimessiah will be too much for the Jewish people to accept. They will turn to the Messiah at last (Matt. 23:39, Zech. 12:11) and be delivered.

Rather than seeing their torment as judgments from God, the world will surely have its own interpretation of the spiritual warfare. In some fashion they will see their religious philosophy triumphing over the prophets of God and will now expect peace: "Get rid of the believers and all shall be well!" Yet the most awesome judgments will follow because the world kills the prophets of God. I believe this is shown in Revelation 13:7, where the Antichrist is given permission to make war against the saints and, in some manner we do not understand, to overcome them. The prophets will show God to be stronger, even the true One, in the face of all the supernatural magicians of the Devil (just as Moses and Aaron showed the superiority of their God over the lame "miracles" of the magicians of Egypt). Yet somehow, there is a brief overcoming by the forces of Satan. Such an overcoming took place in the Holocaust of Hitler through Germany in World War II. The magicians in Egypt deceived the Egyptians for a time. It seemed to the Israelites that they were being overcome by Pharaoh and their slave masters; for a time their slavery was made worse! Ultimately, however, the forces of good triumphed. The overcoming by Satan is temporary and is only perceived from the limited perspective of the seen world. In the unseen world the ultimate victory of Jesus and His people, His Bride, is being prepared. We will fully triumph!

The martyrdom of the prophets leads to an even greater outpouring of God's power. This is the result of true martyrdom—power is released in the spiritual realm! Thus the martyrdom of Chinese saints under Communism led to the greatest church growth since the Church Age began. Martyrdom is similar to the sacrifice of intercessory prayer leading to the victory of the people of God. Thus, the fruition of the sacrifice of the last days martyrs and the intercession of the saints is the great infusion of power that will raise the Church into glory. In translated bodies Christians will return with the Lord for total victory and triumph over Satan and all his forces. Thus the two witnesses stand on their feet, causing all to fear. They are called up to heaven and a great earthquake occurs.

It is possible that this happens at the same time as the rapture of all the saints; the earthquake may parallel the one described in Zechariah 14, in which the Jewish people escape the end-time siege of Jerusalem. In Zechariah 14, we read that after that earthquake, the Lord will come with all His saints to fully defeat the forces of the Antichrist. It is also possible that the resurrection of the two witnesses is a resurrection that precedes and anticipates the full resurrection of the dead and the translation of the saints. *They ascend in the cloud, which I believe is the glory cloud of the Messiah, the cloud seen in the Exodus events.*

The passage concerning the two witnesses (Rev. 11:1-14) precedes the passage on the blowing of the seventh trumpet (vs. 15-19). If we take its placement to be chronologically exact (before the seventh trumpet), then this is not a resurrection that is part of the rapture of the saints in general. If we take the passage as an excursus that somewhat overlaps what is to follow from the blowing of the seventh shofar, then this could be an event that is simultaneous with the rapture of the saints in general. In either case, the resurrection of the prophets is an extraordinary sign for introducing the rapture and resurrection of the saints. My view is the former.

Let us recall that in the excursus or digressive passages, there are overlaps. Chronological progression is not carried through from one such passage to another. This is especially clear in Revelation 12, which includes information from before the birth of Jesus until the last days persecution of Israel and the Church. In the Book of Revelation, there are parallel visions describing the same events from different perspectives. The seals, trumpets and bowls provide us with the chronological pattern. We will later return to the theme of the miraculous escape of the last days people of God. This is an escape of natural, not yet redeemed Israel from Jerusalem, and of the saints from the dimension of earth through the veil into the glory cloud.

Who gives glory to God in these events (11:13)? Could this be Jewish people who now turn to the Messiah? Could it be the Church which soon will follow the witnesses into the glory cloud? Could this be some of the peoples of the world who now see the truth and are beginning to turn to Jesus? All of these, in part or combination, are possibilities.

Revelation 11:15-19 returns us to the progression of trumpets. It is now time for the blowing of the seventh trumpet. This seventh trumpet leads to the rapture of the saints. It is, in my view, the same as the last trumpet foretold in First Thessalonians 4:16-17 and First Corinthians 15:51-52. Thus we find the announcement of full triumph. We will look at this passage more closely in Chapter Five of this volume.

Our next chapter will begin with a view of the excursus passages found in Revelation 12-14. This will fill out the picture from the material presented thus far. We will then return to look at the meaning of the seventh trumpet and what follows from it, as well as the seven bowls of God's wrath which the seventh trumpet introduces. The description of the bowls of wrath is followed by excursus passages which provide more detailed pictures of the forces of evil and the triumph of God's people, the climax of which is found in Revelation 19. Again, there is much overlapping of time sequence in these pictures. At times, the same realities are described in different ways (e.g., the beast in Revelation 13 and 17).

To summarize, in this chapter we have seen the following Passover-Exodus parallels in the Book of Revelation: Many of the plagues of the book are parallel to the Egyptian plagues of the Book of Exodus; the prophets of the last days will announce the plagues as Moses and Aaron did in the days of Pharaoh; the response of the people was similar to that of the Egyptians: they did not turn to God. All of these events are seen on a worldwide scale and will be much more intense than were the events of the Exodus. However, the Exodus events were on a significant scale, since they involved Israel's escape from the greatest power of the region, perhaps of the world at that time. The clear testimony was that the God of Israel was the God of all the earth. Even so, the God of Abraham, Isaac and Jacob, the God of our Lord Jesus the Messiah, will be shown to be the God of all creation in the events of the last days.

CHAPTER III

GOD'S PEOPLE PROTECTED

Please read Revelation chapters 7 and 12.

The Sealing of the One Hundred and Forty-Four Thousand

We read of the four angels at the four corners of the earth who hold the four winds, keeping them from blowing upon the earth in Revelation 7:1-3. This wind intensifies heat and suffering. Another angel having the seal of the living God ascends from the east to command the four angels who have the power to harm the earth and the sea. His command is that they not harm the earth, the sea or the trees until the servants of God are sealed upon their foreheads. The plagues which have occurred and those which follow are not to fall upon the committed believers. *As Israel was protected in the land of Goshen, so believers who are sealed will be protected.* I believe the prophetic words coming forth today concerning cities of refuge in the last days is a true word. Not only will there be individual protection, but God will lead His people to places of protection which will be like Goshen was in Egypt. I mention this because it is in keeping with the theme of the protection of God's people. It is my belief that Jewish people will also be protected by believers in these places of refuge.

Varying interpretations have historically been applied to verse 4. It states, "And I heard the number of those who were sealed. One hundred and forty-four thousand of all the tribes of the children of Israel were sealed...." Does this mean that only people of Jewish or Israelite descent are sealed? Some have taught that this means the Church is no longer on the earth during the tribulation; only Israel remains of the people of God! We would therefore have a book of the Bible that was written for believers to read (22:6,9-10), but that does not apply directly to any in the Bride of the Messiah!

Others see the 144,000 as symbolic of the Church. We are told that the number is clearly symbolic: 12 X 12 X 10 X 10 X 10 = 144,000. Twelve is the number of the tribes of Israel and the apostles. Ten is for completeness, and three is for God (ten is multiplied three times). Furthermore, we are told that 12,000 are listed from each tribe in verses 5-8. However, the tribe of Dan is absent from this roll. Was this because Dan first led Israel toward idolatry, as recorded in the Book of Judges? Yet we know that today, although each tribe is represented, they are indistinguishable. Therefore, some say the twelve tribes are symbolic of the Body of believers; we are told that this passage refers to spiritual Israel, not to natural Israel.

I do not agree with this view. First of all, I do not believe that the Bible ever uses the terms "Israel" or "Jew" as terms for believers. The scriptural term for believers who are not of Jewish birth is "spiritual seed [children] of Abraham" (Gal. 3:29). Galatians 6:16 and Romans 2 are used to support the spiritual Israel terminology, but I believe this is not correct, and that this terminology is confusing. Both passages, I believe, refer to Jews or Israelites who are born again and following the pattern of apostolic teaching. I believe that it is the case here as well. Yes, the number 144,000 is symbolic. However, it is the number of the saved remnant of Israel in the last days. It may refer only to the saved remnant in the land, or to just the men of this saved remnant, or to the saved of world Jewry.

Personally, I believe the saved of world Jewry during this period will be larger than this number, which will be either a tithe or double tithe of the Jewish people. This would make the number of redeemed Jews between 1.2 and 3 million. However, this is a prophetic sense on my part. I am not saying, "Thus saith the Lord." I believe that the 144,000 could be both symbolic and close to a literal number of the believing Jewish men in the land of Israel. The Israelites in the Sinai desert were counted in such a way. With women and children, their number was well over the 600,000 recorded. We will have to see the fulfillment as it comes. The passage is prophetic concerning a great company of witnesses who are Jewish in the land of Israel; this is the saved remnant of Israel!

Paul was concerned about seeing a remnant of Israel saved as a prelude to Israel's full acceptance of the Lord (see Romans 11:14-15). The saved remnant of Israel is both part of national Israel or world Jewry, and is the

Jewish membership of the Body of the Messiah. Will God actually see that 12,000 are saved from each tribe? This is possible. The descent of the Israelites is known only to Him. Some things we see as being symbolic will happen with far more literal fulfillment than we now realize. However, *although the sealing is specifically applied to the saved remnant of Israel here, I believe the principle of sealing is universal among believers.* This is the implication of Revelation 9:4, where the locusts were commanded

> *"not to harm the grass of the earth, or any green thing, or any tree, but only those men who do not have the seal of God on their foreheads."*

The saints from all nations are clearly distinguished from the 144,000 in Revelation 7:9-17. The first part of the chapter speaks of Israel, the second part of the universal people of God from all nations. Evidence for this interpretation is found in that the second group in Revelation 7 is described in quite different terms:

> *...a great multitude which no one could number, of all nations, tribes, peoples, and tongues, standing before the throne and before the Lamb, clothed with white robes, with palm branches in their hands....*

> Revelation 7:9

These cry out in worship, extolling God the Father and the Lamb. As they worship, the four living creatures and the 24 elders fall down and worship as well. These are not specifically described as martyrs or as people who have died. This picture is a vision of the Body of the Messiah which is described in Ephesians as "seated with

Him in heavenly places." Through the presence of the Holy Spirit, the believers individually and corporately transcend space and are fully present before the throne of God. Although this is not a reality presently seen by the physical eye, it is real nonetheless.

The white robes are symbols of purity and of priestly ministry. The worship of the saints is joined by the worship of those in heaven. What an extraordinary picture! In the midst of the tribulation, the saints are in worship and are caught up to the throne. Our experience of this reality depends on the quality of our worship in unity. The angels and elders join in worship, singing, **"Thanksgiving and honor and power and might be to our God forever and ever"** (v. 12b).

John is told that this great multitude represents those who have come out of the great tribulation and washed their robes white in the blood of the Lamb. This is a picture of the last days Church of God. The time span covers all the saints who will live through this period. I believe this is a great picture of our unity and purity in the last days, for which Yeshua prayed (John 17:20-26) and which Paul predicted would come about (Eph. 4:11-16). This people serves God before the throne day and night. This is a worshiping, intercessory people. The Lamb dwells among them, and they are protected from the plagues. Again, it is not only the Jewish remnant that is protected, but all true believers are delivered from hunger, thirst, the scorching sun and the beasts that plague the earth. Their destiny is to experience great comfort, for God will wipe away all their tears.

Revelation 9:4 reiterates the fact that the supernatural locusts are told they must not harm the men who have the seal of God on their foreheads. This is part of God's plan of protection for His people.

Additional pictures of God's protection are found in Revelation chapters 11 and 12. Revelation 11, as we have seen, gives us the account of the two prophetic witnesses of the last days, paralleling Moses and Aaron in Egypt. As Moses and Aaron did, they prophetically announce the plagues. The protection of all God's witnesses is typified by these prophetic leaders. Verse 5 tells us that any who want to kill them experience the judgment of God: Fire proceeds out of their mouths and devours their enemies. The word of God spoken brings swift judgments. Such will be the power of God's prophetic people. Indeed, God's people will be protected by being prophetically led.

However, the witnesses are killed in Revelation 11:7. We also have a picture of the martyrs from the tribulation in chapter 5. This raises the question of the extent of God's protection during these difficult days. I believe that as Jesus said that no one had power over Him, but that He would lay down His life, so is the situation with the two witnesses and the various segments of the restored Body of the Messiah of the last days. We will be fully protected in many ways: in Goshens of God or protected cities, through supernatural acts of God and in many other ways. When people sought to kill Jesus, either supernatural power or circumstances from God prevented them. Yet there was a point at which God the Father desired that Jesus lay down His life. As Jesus taught, in the ultimate sense, not a hair of our heads will be lost. However, in the proximate sense, some will be called upon by God to lay down their lives. This martyrdom, as we before stated, releases awesome spiritual power in the heavenlies and on earth. It looks as though Satan and the Antichrist are overcoming the saints; but this is only in the sight of natural man. In reality, the blood of the martyrs releases the power of ultimate victory. It has been well stated that the blood of the martyrs is the seed of the Church. Indeed, history proves that martyrdom in large numbers gives powerful testimony to Jesus. Such "seed" has often led to the greatest revivals of the Church and large success in evangelism. This has recently been proven in China and other lands of oppression.

The Woman, the Child, Israel and the Church
(Rev. 12:1-17)

Revelation 12 is an excursus that gives us a picture of the sweep of history concerning Israel, the Messiah and the Church. Let us look at this passage more closely.

The great sign is a woman, clothed with the sun, the moon under her feet and a garland of twelve stars on her head. We see the meaning of the symbols as follows: To be clothed with the sun is to be clothed with the light of God. Dominion is represented in the position of the moon under the woman's feet. Her regal standing is shown in the garland of twelve stars on her head. The number of the stars correctly gives rise to the thought that they represent the twelve tribes of Israel. The woman is in labor with a child, according to verse 2.

Verse 3 introduces us to another sign in heaven: a great, fiery red dragon with seven heads, ten horns and seven diadems on his heads. The image of the beast reminds us of the beast with ten horns at the end of Daniel 7. The number seven gives a sense of perfect or complete authority; ten also stands as a number of completeness. The rulership of either progressive emperors or subrulers of various provinces could be represented. The dragon is Satan, the old serpent represented in Isaiah 27 as the leviathan whom God will punish. (See Revelation 20:17.) However, the dragon's last manifestation of power will be similar to its manifestation in the first century. The parallel to the days of the Roman Empire and the last days is noteworthy. The dragon manifests himself through political leadership in the human realm.

Israel's lot throughout history has been persecution by the dragon. This has included both the nation as a whole and the Messianic Jewish remnant.

The reference to a third of the stars being thrown to earth reminds us that Satan took a third of the angels with him in his rebellion. Stars can represent angelic leaders, human leaders or both in scriptural symbolism.

Israel, the woman, is ready to give birth. The dragon awaits this birth and stands ready to devour the Child. This Child is none other than Jesus the Messiah, who is to rule "all nations with a rod of iron." Jesus rules with His Church, so the reference to ruling with a rod of iron is applied to the Church in Revelation 2:26-27. It is clear that Satan was seeking to destroy Jesus and His work from the time of His birth until His death on the cross. First, Herod was Satan's instrument. Herod commanded the slaughter of the babies in the environs of Bethlehem. Religious leaders sought to kill Him before His time. Lastly, in the Garden of Gethsemane, I believe Satan attempted to kill the Lord. However, God protected Jesus. After His resurrection, Jesus ascended to the Father or, as it says in verse 5, He was "caught up to God and to His throne."

The woman fled into the wilderness to a place of protection prepared by God. This wilderness time is described as twelve hundred and sixty days, or three and one half years. Some have taken this to be a literal time period for the worst part of the tribulation. Half of seven years is a level of tribulation that is intense, but only half the full measure of tribulation suffering.

The picture given in verse 4 is expanded in verses 7-9. Here we see the war between the faithful angels of God and the fallen angels of Satan. Michael and his hosts prevail and his angels are cast out of the heaven of God to earth (the lower atmosphere). Satan, the one who makes false accusations against the brethren, has been cast down.

We find here another image of the protection of the followers of Jesus during the tribulation.

"And they overcame him by the blood of the Lamb and by the word of their testimony, and they did not love their lives to the death" (v. 11).

Appeal to our righteousness on the basis of the blood of the Lamb silences the accuser and opens us to the power of God to resist the Devil and to cause him to flee. A woe is pronounced upon the earth because it is the scene of Satan's activity whereby he seeks to thwart the plan of God and destroy mankind. This occurs throughout history, but intensifies in the last days when Satan's time is very short.

The dragon persecutes the woman (v. 13). Corporate Israel and the Messianic Jewish community are ultimately protected in the wilderness and survive the attacks of the Devil. "Times, time and half a time" (v. 14) is often seen as three and one half years. This is a repetition of the information in verse 6. The woman is protected from the floods of water that are poured out against her. This is not to say that Israel has not suffered awesome persecution and destruction, but in the ultimate sense, the woman is protected from destruction and survives.

The Body of the Messiah is portrayed in verse 17. The dragon is enraged that he cannot overcome the woman, Israel. Therefore,

"he went to make war with the rest of her offspring, who keep the commandments of God and have the testimony of Jesus Christ."

The Church is the offspring of Israel; she is a Jewish-rooted people. Israel and the Church represent two parts of God's unified plan for world redemption. Satan rages against both; the purposes of both are one and intertwined, as is clearly seen in Romans 11. Therefore, the same Devil who seeks to destroy Israel seeks to destroy the Church. This has been true throughout history, but will be especially so at the end of this transitional age.

However, once again the theme of this chapter proves true. As God ultimately protects Israel, so He protects His faithful remnant of Messianic Jews and their brothers and sisters from all nations in lands of Goshen, through His supernatural power at work in them, and by the blood of the Lamb. There will be cities of refuge and areas where God's people are in control. There is ultimate protection even for those called to martyrdom.

Not a hair of their heads will be lost. Indeed, His faithful people will rule and reign with Him in complete victory.

We conclude by again noting that **another theme of the Exodus** in the Torah is **intensified** and brought to **worldwide dimensions: God's people are supernaturally protected.**

CHAPTER IV

ANTIMESSIAH—THE LAST DAYS' PHARAOH

The Book of Revelation presents a picture of the leaders of the end times who oppose the people of God. The central figure of such leaders is the Antichrist. His response to God's people is similar to the response of Pharaoh to God's people in Egypt. Not only are we given a glimpse of the Antichrist himself, but we also see the false prophet who is the contrast to the true prophets in Revelation 11. Satan, the Devil, in the form of the dragon; the image of the beast or Antichrist; the harlot, the image of false religion; and Babylon, the image of the ungodly kingdom are all portrayed in Revelation.

The Beast from the Sea (Rev. 13:1-10)

The fact that the beast comes from the sea is symbolic of his arising from the peoples (Rev. 13:1). Its seven heads and ten horns are reminiscent of the Book of Daniel (chapter 7). Seven is the number of perfection and ten of completeness. We are seeing the perfect completeness of evil rule. Again, the ten horns could represent rulership over nations centered in either ten symbolic or ten literal nations. The beast is swift like a leopard, strong like a bear and boasts authority as a lion roars. His power and authority come from the dragon, the Devil.

Many have speculated concerning the mortal wound on one of the heads of the beast. Some have been prompted to see this in terms of a literal Roman emperor, with the seven heads being a succession of emperors. Thus the beast is not one ruler, but a succession of rulers of the same spirit. The one wounded is either the last in the series or one of the series. However, because of the ultimacy of these chapters in the Book of Revelation, I believe we should wait for more light which will be given by God during the events yet to come. It is not yet time to pin this down. Prophetic speculators have not been wanting who have sought to identify the wounded head. Some have seen it as prophetic of Hitler's injury after the bomb attack which failed to kill him. Some have even seen it as manifest in the near-fatal wound suffered by Pope John Paul II after the attempt upon his life a few years ago, even though the injury was not on his head. Heads upon the beast represent different persons. Paul makes it clear in Second Thessalonians 2 that there will be an ultimate world ruler designated "Antichrist." Do they marvel at the beast because of a healing from the wound? The text is not clear, but this is possible.

Not only do the people worship the beast, but they directly worship Satan, the dragon who gives power to the beast. The fact that the beast boasts great things (as ancient Pharaohs and other Middle-Eastern kings) reminds us of the little horn who so boasts in Daniel 7. Again, we see many rulers who fit the description of Daniel 7, beginning with Antiochus IV in the second century B.C. The beast blasphemes, or speaks in boastful terms concerning his position while coming against that which is holy or of God. Again we see the time frame of 42 months (three and one half years) for his dominating rulership.

Although the Devil and those given to him engage the saints in war, both spiritually and physically, all such tests are ultimately under the control of God for our purification. The beast is given authority to make war and to overcome the saints. This does not, in my view, mean that he destroys the Body of believers, but that his persecution leads to the martyrdom of many saints and his *apparent* victory over the saints. This was the case with the Chinese communist attack on the church of China. Yet we now know that the Chinese church has been triumphant and has multiplied beyond any other church in history! This passage in no way contradicts the fact that a great harvest will be gathered in the last days. However, the victory of the people of God, after they have apparently been overcome, will be historically unique.

Verses 7-8 tell us that the beast achieves great world domination over every "tribe, tongue, and nation." Humanity is divided into two: those whose names are written in the Lamb's Book of Life, and all others. Yet verse 10 assures us that God's judgment will ultimately prevail. The law of sowing and reaping will prove true. Confidence in God will produce "patience and the faith of the saints" (v. 9).

The False Prophet (Rev. 13:11-17)

The second beast arises from the land. His two horns symbolize strength or authority. It is possible that they represent a double portion of authority, or there may be two prophets carrying the leadership of false prophets. There will be many false prophets in the last days. The New Age movement provides us with a picture of a subtle but sinister religious movement with its own cadre of false prophets. However, just as the people of God are represented in two prominent prophets (Revelation 11) paralleling Moses and Aaron in ancient Egypt, so this beast represents false prophets of the last days. As did the false prophets of Pharaoh, this beast performs signs. But his signs are much greater than those performed by the magicians of Egypt. He prophesies to the nations to encourage them to worship the first beast, the Antichrist. Signs and wonders are vividly described.

"He performs great signs, so that he even makes fire come down from heaven on the earth in the sight of men. And he deceives those who dwell on the earth by those signs which he was granted to do in the sight of the beast, telling those who dwell on the earth to make an image to the beast who was wounded by the sword and lived."

Revelation 13:13-14

This beast even causes the image of the idol of the first beast to speak and has those who do not worship the Antichrist killed. It almost reminds us of a robot-type figure with a memory link sufficient to know who is not signing on with the evil one and can give the orders for execution. This worship is professed by taking upon oneself the mark of the beast. Ancient societies had marks and incisions for slaves and religious rituals. Even so, the people of God are instructed in the Torah to bind His Law on their heads and hands. However, modern computer technology has rightly caused some to think that this could imply new and more frightening dimensions in the last days.

The Number 666

The number of the beast which all must take is 66C. Great pains have been taken to identify this number by adding up the numerical values of the letters in various names and by identifying the number with ancient emperors or contemporary figures. That 666 is the first part of the numeric series of today's bar codes, which are used in computer scanning in many transactions, has caused great concern. Surely we can see the possibilities of such controls in our computerized society. It is indeed amazing that bar codes begin with the number 666. However, the speculations for specific identifications have yielded little fruit. The number six in Hebrew numerology is the number of man. Multiplied by three it is a representation of man apart from God, building his own kingdom and authority; three sixes are the false human trinity seeking to replace the triune God of the Bible.

The excursus of Revelation 13 on the Antichrist and the false prophet is followed by a picture of the 144,000 of the tribes of Israel. The content of Revelation 14 fits better in the following chapter. Chapters 15 and 16 provide material connected with the completion of the seventh trumpet in the outpouring of the seven bowls of God's wrath. Therefore, we shall next study chapters 17 and 18, which recount further visions of the last days enemies of God's Kingdom.

Excursus: The Scarlet Woman, the Beast and the Fall of Babylon (Revelation 17,18)

This passage begins with the picture of a scarlet woman sitting on a beast who is described in the same terms as the beast of the first part of Revelation 13. However, chapters 17 and 18 provide us with an expanded picture of what the people of God are up against in the last days with a clear prophecy of the defeat of the forces of evil. (This is not provided in Revelation 13.) Clearly, the beast's overcoming the saints is apparent, not ultimate. The woman is arrayed with great jewels. She is "Mystery, Babylon the Great, the Mother of Harlots and of the abominations of the earth" (17:5). This woman is drunk with the blood of the martyrs. She is the representation of religious, economic and political power conjoined into one ungodly, wicked world system.

Further information is given here about the beast. Its seven heads represent the seven hills, a clear reference to Rome. Roman power, at the time this book was written, was the Babylonian system of the day. The seven kings represent the succession of ungodly emperors. The seventh has not yet come (v. 10). The numbers become complex here. Are we speaking of a succession of known emperors during the first century? Many have thought so and have tried to give an identification. Yet the focus of the book ultimately stretches beyond the first century to the very end of this transitional age. An eighth is described that arises out of the seventh. Is this none other than the final representative of the whole series? I believe it is.

We herein find as well that the ten horns represent lesser rulers who control various kingdoms under the beast. By supporting the beast they give him power and authority.

In chapter 13 we are told that the beast makes war against the saints and overcomes them. However, this is an incomplete picture. The saints are joined to the Messiah Jesus. Ultimately, the beast's war against the saints is war against the Messiah.

> *"These [kings] will make war with the Lamb, and the Lamb will overcome them, for he is Lord of lords and King of kings; and those who are with Him are called, chosen, and faithful."*

> Revelation 17:14

The harlot sits over the waters, or "peoples, multitudes, nations, and tongues." This whole system becomes dominant over the earth just before the last battle.

Strangely, verse 17 tells us that the ten kings will hate the harlot and make her desolate and "eat her flesh and burn her with fire." The woman is a harlot because she is the image of spiritual adultery, or unfaithfulness to God the Father, Creator of all. The woman is described as the chief city of the world system (v. 18). I believe this refers to the fact that the rulers of this world, as well as rulers of the false system, have within themselves the seeds of their own destruction. Some have seen contemporary

New York as a good representation of the false kingdom of this world. The humanist systems, the perversions and the initiatives taken in this city have perverted the whole country. Yet the city itself is rotting through the seeds of destruction inherent in its false philosophies and behaviors.

The announcement of the fall of the false city and its system of evil is a source of rejoicing for the saints. A bright angel with great authority announces the destruction (18:1-2). The description of Babylon, the great harlot, is clearly a full description of decadence.

> *"Babylon the great is fallen, is fallen, and has become a habitation of demons, a prison for every foul spirit, and a cage for every unclean and hated bird! For all of the nations have drunk of the wine of the wrath of her fornication, the kings of the earth have committed fornication with her, and the merchants of the earth have become rich through the abundance of her luxury."*

Revelation 18:2-3

God's people are called to come out of her (v. 4). We are to be separate from the world system, living according to the holy standards of God by the power of the Spirit. This call to holiness is necessary if we are to avoid the plagues of God's judgments. It is crucial that we realize *that protection from the plagues in the Goshens of God is for God's holy people.* Carnal, worldly, compromising "believers" will not be protected from the plagues of the last days.

Verses seven and eight make it clear that the judgment on the harlot will be swift, even as in a single day. She will be burned by fire. These last verses introduce us to the wrath of God on Babylon and fit the meaning of God's bowls of wrath, as we shall see.

CHAPTER V

THE EXODUS RAPTURE

Although chapter 13 of the Book of Revelation left us with the apparent victory of the Antichrist over the saints, the rest of the book makes it clear that the victory of the saints is assured. Although circumstances will look dark, the spiritual reality will be that the saved from all the nations of the earth will be at their greatest point of holiness, unity and power since the first century. The purity and unity of the people of God is expressed through intense intercession. Having completed its Kingdom gospel witness and having been a light to Israel, the people of God will stand in a position similar to that of the children of Israel before they crossed the Red Sea.

As Israel at the sea seemed soon to be defeated by the advancing forces of Pharaoh, so will the Body of believers seem to be crushed in the last days. A worldwide attack will be advancing upon them. Israel will also see the last invasion of the forces of the Antichrist. As Zechariah 14 states, all nations will come upon Jerusalem. Half of the city will go into exile; the women will be raped; destruction from the forces of the Antichrist will be upon the city. It will look dark indeed for both Israel and the Body of Christ.

For believers in Jesus, this situation will be such a clear fulfillment of biblical prophecy that there will be a unified cry of intercession such as has never been on the face of the earth. Believers from every nation will be crying out for the return of Jesus. "Maranatha," they will cry, "Come, Lord!" I believe they will also yearn for the salvation and deliverance of Israel. This unity of holiness, faith and intercession will be met by the glorious appearing of the Lord Jesus. Israel was hemmed in by the sea, but Moses responded in faith. He stretched forth his rod and the waters parted. The Israelites escaped, but the troops of Pharaoh were drowned in the sea in the wrath of God. *Even so, the people of God will escape from this dimension of earthly existence through and into the glory cloud and on to the other side.* This is the rapture of the saints (I Thess. 4:16-17, I Cor. 15:51-54).

The last days began when the Spirit was poured out at Pentecost. I see the last days metaphorically as like the World Series in baseball. The last of the last days is the seventh game of the series. The overcoming by the beast (Revelation 13) is his seeming lead in that final game. The score is six to three. The home team, the Body of Believers, is at the plate. There are two outs. Through the power of the Spirit, we will get a hit, a walk and a bunt single. The bases will be loaded. It is at this moment that the Devil will face the Player-Manager, Yeshua the Messiah. Jesus will come to bat and hit the grand slam home run to give us victory. The return of Jesus effects the full manifestation of the sons of God (Romans 8). The saints will come with Him (Zech. 14:5). There will be a continuing series of events at His return, when His feet will stand on the Mount of Olives (Zech. 14:3). This is like the home team's runners circling the bases and touching home plate.

These are the ninth inning hits that load the bases: the Body of Believers completes its worldwide Kingdom witness; the Body of Believers, including the saved remnant of Israel, witnesses and prays Israel into the place of considering that calling on Jesus might be the key to her salvation; and finally Israel calls upon the Name of Jesus! Israel's leaders will say, "Blessed is He who comes in the name of the Lord" (Matt. 23:39). Zechariah 14 shows that the Jewish people in Jerusalem also have an exodus escape through the valley. The escape route is caused by the earthquake.

With this introduction, it is now appropriate to look at the chapters of the Book of Revelation that deal with this exodus rapture into the glory cloud.

The Sounding of the Seventh Shofar (Rev. 11:15-19)

Scripture tells us that the rapture of the saints will occur at the blowing of the last shofar (I Cor. 15:51-53, I Thess. 4:16-18). The sounding of the seventh shofar in Revelation 11:10 is clearly the same as the last shofar in the other mentioned passages. It heralds the ultimate victory of God and His people.

Then the seventh angel sounded: And there were loud voices in heaven, saying, "The kingdoms of this

world have become the kingdoms of our Lord and of
His Christ, and He shall reign forever and ever!"
And the twenty-four elders who sat before God on
their thrones fell on their faces and worshiped God,
saying: "We give You thanks, O Lord God Almighty,
the One who is and who was and who is to come, be-
cause You have taken Your great power and reigned.
The nations were angry, and Your wrath has come,
and the time of the dead, that they should be judged,
and that You should reward Your servants the
prophets and the saints, and those who fear Your
name, small and great, and should destroy those who
destroy the earth." Then the temple of God was
opened in heaven, and the ark of His covenant was
seen in His temple. And there were lightnings,
noises, thunderings, an earthquake, and great hail.

Revelation 11:15-19

I quote the entire passage because of its great significance relative to the theme of this chapter. That the seventh trumpet announces the Kingdom of God in fulness and judgment is a clear indication that the mighty appearing of Jesus is being announced. Indeed, this is the time of His wrath and the establishment of His reign. This takes place with the rapture of the saints, even when the saints are rewarded (v. 18).

The seventh shofar brings this transitional age to its climax; seven again denotes perfection or completion. (Some Christians believe, as do the rabbis, that spiritual time is divided into seven thousand years: two thousand years from Adam to Abraham, two thousand from Abraham to Messiah's first coming, two thousand in this transitional age, and one thousand years of the Millennial Sabbath Age.) The saved representatives of Israel, with the whole Body of Believers, worship God. Great power is seen at His throne. Again, the imagery before the throne of God with the Ark in the heavenly Temple finds its parallel in the Old Tesament. Recall the awesome power of God in lightning, thunder and earthquake on Mount Sinai after the Exodus, when the Law was given. Indeed, the glory cloud rested upon the mountain; this cloud is the transitional plane between the dimensions of heaven and earth. Looking into the glory cloud, we see the throne of God. Therefore the manifestations in verse 19 of this chapter and in Exodus chapter 19 are similar.

The Resurrection of the Two Prophet Witnesses
(Rev. 11:11-14)

The resurrection of the saints takes place when Jesus returns. Some have therefore seen the resurrection of the two prophet witnesses in chapter 11 as signalling the rapture of the saints. This is especially so among those who see the witnesses as symbolic of the people of God and not as individuals. Although I see the prophets as representatives of last days prophets, it seems likely to me that there will be two leading prophets as a focal point. Because Revelation chapter 11 is an excursus, it is possible that the ascension of the two prophets could take place simultaneously with the rapture of the saints. Though the Book of Revelation is not consistently chronological, I sense that it is better to see this excursus as preceding the rapture because it comes between the blowing of the sixth and seventh trumpets. There is a logic in the placement of the excursus passages in the book that has some relationship to chronology. This event might even be a sign that pushes Israel toward calling out to Jesus, "Blessed is He who comes in the name of the Lord!" (Matt. 23:39)

The resurrection of the two witnesses is not an instant translation to Heaven, for they will stand on their feet and great fear will fall on those who see them. Then will come the voice that calls them into the glory cloud, "Come up here." Their enemies will see them. This is followed by the great earthquake in which a tenth of the city will fall. This could be the beginning of tremors that will eventually lead to the splitting of the Mount of Olives as part of the events that take place at the return of the Lord (Zech. 14). If this prophecy is to be fulfilled in a literal fashion, surely the saints will know that their rapture is immediately at hand.

Another proof of the seventh trumpet being the trumpet that announces and immediately precedes the rapture of the saints and the return of the Lord is seen in Revelation 10:5-7.

And the angel whom I saw standing on the sea and on the land lifted up his hand to heaven and swore by Him who lives forever and ever, who created heaven and the things that are in it, the earth and the things that are in it, and the sea and the things that are in it, that there should be delay no longer, but in the days of the sounding of the seventh angel, when he is about to sound, the mystery of God would be finished, as He declared to His servants the prophets.

"Mystery," in New Testament writing, primarily means that which was previously hidden but is now revealed. In Pauline writings, this mystery is the Church, the Body of believers. The revelation given to Paul was that in this transitional age, God was calling out from all nations a Bride who would rule in the age to come. In this Bride Jew and Gentile are one. The completion of the mystery means that the full number from all the nations, Jew and Gentile, have come into this Body, which has completed its pre-resurrection or pre-rapture task. The Bride is a reflection or foreshadowing of the age to come, when Israel and the nations shall be in one worldwide **commonwealth of Israel** under the rule of the Messiah.

The coming of Jesus brings both redemption and wrath. Chapter fourteen provides us with pictures that lead up to the actual description of the rapture.

A Vision of the 144,000 (Rev. 14:1-5)

There is much debate over this picture of the 144,000. Again, we know that the number twelve is the number of Israel and ten the number of completion. (10 X 10 X 10) X (12 X 12) = 144,000. These are not explicitly revealed to be the saved remnant of Israel, but are said to be those redeemed from among men, the firstfruits. In other words, more salvation or redemption is to come as more will be harvested into the Kingdom of God, especially in the Age to Come. Some have therefore said that this is a picture of the Church. Their virgin status denotes spiritual purity, not necessarily an unmarried state. Because the 144,000 are described as the saved remnant of Israel in chapter seven, I believe it is best to see this group as such, the Jewish members of the Body of the Messiah. Again, their worship ascends and joins with the worship of those in Heaven. How glorious that the blood of Jesus and His sanctifying power can cause human beings to be described as "without fault." They are firstfruits because Jewish believers are the firstfruits of the harvest out of all the nations. They reflect the state of all true believers.

The Father's name is on their foreheads. The people of God are marked, not only the people of the Antichrist. The people having the mark of the beast will have to go through the bowls of God's wrath, but not those who have the Father's mark (Rev. 14:9).

Proclamations by Three Angels (Rev. 14:6-13)

The pictures in this section prepare us for the rapture. As the six trumpets are past, it is now time to choose the everlasting Gospel or to suffer the wrath of God. The announcement of Babylon's fall is part of the judgment of the wrath of God on the kingdoms of this world. This fall is more vividly described in chapters 17 and 18. Many statements in the Book of Revelation find their expansion in other passages. The warning not to partake of the mark of the beast in verses 9-10 speak of suffering the wrath of God, a wrath of torment with fire and brimstone before God's holy angels. I do not believe this speaks of everlasting damnation, but rather of the experience of the bowls of God's judgments in chapter 16. Of course, those who ultimately refuse the offer of redemption experience a final separation from God and the wrath of His everlasting judgment. That the smoke of their torment ascends forever speaks of the permanence of the judgment of those who even refuse God's redemption when the bowls of His wrath are poured out (Rev. 14:10-11). God's wrath on earth foreshadows the judgment of hell and the lake of fire.

Two greatly comforting words are given that apply to all saints who suffer persecution for the Lord. First we are told that this is the patience of the saints. They know that God will ultimately bring full and fair judgment. Their witness is part of gathering the harvest of the last days. Furthermore, if they die in the Lord, they know that they will soon be coming with Him in resurrection bodies. Their works of faith follow them as eternal rewards. The fruit that remains from our lives will be as an eternal crown of glory.

The Exodus Rapture: Into the Glory Cloud
(Rev. 14:14-16)

Finally the moment has come; the seventh trumpet has sounded and the harvest of the saints, the rapture, is about to take place. As described in Matthew 24 and parallel synoptic passages, the Lord returns to gather His harvest from all over the earth.

Then the sign of the Son of Man will appear in heaven, and then all of the tribes of the earth will mourn, and they will see the Son of Man coming on the clouds of heaven with power and great glory. And He will send His angels with a great sound of a trumpet, and they will gather together His elect from the four winds, from one end of heaven to the other.

Matthew 24:30-31

In a sense, the rapture of the saints parallels the gathering of the children of Israel back to their land, that is, those who are still scattered.

So it shall be in that day. That the great trumpet will be blown; they will come, who are about to perish in the land of Assyria, and they who are outcasts in the land of Egypt, and shall worship the Lord in the holy mount at Jerusalem.

Isaiah 27:13

These pictures surely prepare us for the wonderful description found in Revelation 14:14-16.

And I looked, and behold, a white cloud, and on the cloud sat One like the Son of Man, having on His head a golden crown, and in his hand a sharp sickle. And another angel came out of the temple, crying with a loud voice to Him who sat on the cloud, "Thrust in Your sickle and reap, for the time has come for You to reap, for the harvest of the earth is ripe." So He who sat on the cloud thrust in His sickle on the earth, and the earth was reaped.

The phrase "rapture of the saints" has produced significant controversy. This is because some who do not believe in a Pre-tribulation rapture (seven years before Jesus actually comes to earth) think the term "rapture" means "pre-tribulation rapture." It does not; it simply refers to believers being "caught up" to meet the Lord at His coming. In this sense, all believers I know believe in the rapture.

The victory of the rapture of the saints in the return of the Lord assures the downfall of Satan, the beast and the kingdoms of this world. We are raised into glory to come with Him as His armies. We return to rule with Him and to establish His Kingdom in all the earth! We will have escaped the forces of the Antichrist in a mighty exodus through the glory cloud to the other side.

CHAPTER VI

THE WRATH OF THE LAMB AND HIS ARMIES

We ended our last chapter with Revelation 14:16, a great picture of the harvest of the saints. However, this is not the only harvest presented here. This chapter also foretells the harvest of the wicked for the judgment of God.

The Harvest of the Wicked (Rev. 14:17-20)

In these verses we read of an angel with a sharp sickle coming from the Temple of God in Heaven. This angel is to gather a harvest as well. This harvest is to "...gather the clusters of the vine of the earth, for her grapes are fully ripe." The vine of the earth is gathered and thrown into the winepress of the wrath of God. As grapes represent blood in sacrificial ceremony, so the wrath of God squeezes out the blood, or the life, of those who experience it. The quantity of blood outside the city reaches to the horses' bridles.

This particular passage is an introduction to what follows. A worldwide judgment produces much death. The description of the amount of blood is metaphorical, as if the blood were to be gathered in one locality. However, the winepress of wrath covers the earth.

The wrath of God comes after the rapture as the saints are returning with the Lord. Various dimensions of this wrath are described in different pictures. First is the seven bowls of God's wrath, which give a picture of plagues and other types of judgments poured out on all the earth. There are two other pictures which, I believe, will be fulfilled simultaneously with this: the final fall of Babylon and the destruction of the armies of the Antichrist, whose forces include soldiers from all nations. *As Pharaoh's armies were drowned in the Red Sea in God's wrath, so the Antichrist is drowned in the judgments of God poured out at the return of Jesus with His victorious armies.*

The Seven Bowls of God's Wrath (Revelation 15, 16)

In Revelation chapter fifteen we see the seven angels with the seven last plagues come out of the heavenly Temple. This will complete the wrath of God. Verse 2 also gives a picture of the victory of the saints: John sees a sea of glass mingled with fire upon which the saints who have the victory over the beast, his image and his mark stand. They have the harps of God. Is this a picture of the saints after the rapture? They will be ordered into ranks to soon return with the Lord.

The saints sing the song of Moses and the Lamb in verses 3-4. There is no false separation between the revelation of Moses and the revelation of Jesus. They are one and lead to the ultimate fulfillment of the prophetic hope that "...all nations shall come and worship before You, for Your judgments have been manifested" (v. 4b).

The Temple is filled with the power of the glory of God. No one may enter it until the plagues are complete. We again see the parallel to the Book of Exodus, wherein the glory of God filled the Tabernacle so that the priests could not minister.

After this glory is revealed, the charge is given to pour out the bowls of the wrath of God. *The first bowl* issues in foul and loathsome sores upon those who had the mark of the beast. Again these plagues remind us of Exodus plagues. However, the exact nature of the progression is different, because in this case, I believe, the saints are not on earth.

I believe that the seven bowls of God's wrath are given in a very brief period of time. This period is symbolized in the Jewish calendar as the time between the feast of the blowing of the trumpet (Rosh Hashana) and the holy day of Yom Kippur. This is a ten-day period. It is possible that the period of the outpouring of the wrath of God is literally that short. However, the ten-day period of the calendar may be symbolic of this last brief, but most intense, period of judgment.

With *the second bowl*, the sea becomes blood and the living creatures in the sea die. *The third bowl* also turns water to blood, in this case rivers and springs of water. Because the wicked have shed the blood of saints, their penalty is to drink blood. Whether this is literal or is symbolic of putrid red waters, the penalty would be fitting.

The fourth bowl brings scorching heat from the sun. A major change in weather patterns could easily cause this. If other calamities disrupt electric power, men could be faced with a situation with no possibility of relief. Yet men are in such deception and sin that they blaspheme the Name of God instead of repenting. How could this be possible? Surely the Devil knows his time is short. Perhaps he convinces the world that good is evil and evil is good, leading men to curse God as a false god, that he might be empowered to bring deliverance. Of course, Satan will not be able to remove these plagues any more than Pharaoh's magicians could remove the plagues of his day. Yet could not mankind be deceived into cursing God as the solution?

A picture of this period is found in Isaiah. Some passages are so pertinent that it is well worth mentioning them and directing the reader to further study. In Isaiah 26:28-27:1, we read that God calls His people into their chambers to hide themselves until the indignation is past. We read that the Lord "comes out of His place to punish the inhabitants of the earth for their iniquity." The Lord, with His "severe sword...will punish Leviathan, the fleeing serpent."

In Isaiah 60:2-3 we read of the period of the second coming in these terms:

> *For behold, the darkness shall cover the earth, and deep darkness the people; but the Lord will arise over you, and His glory will be seen upon you. The Gentiles shall come to your light, and kings to the brightness of your rising."*

The fifth bowl brings darkness over the earth. In the people's great pain, God is blasphemed again. Is this such a strange response? The plagues of human existence are sure marks that the human race is under judgment and in need of redemption. Such plagues are suffered corporately by humanity, not always as a result of individual sin and judgment. All such judgments should lead mankind to repent and to seek the mercy of God. It is a result of sowing and reaping. Yet the response of much of humanity is to debate the problem of evil. How can God be good and allow such human suffering? How blind the race of man is! Rather the conclusion should be that man must be exceedingly wicked if God, who is good, allows such suffering and pain. If we could see in the light of God's righteousness, we would find that the level of human suffering could have been much worse, but God has been exceedingly merciful and patient, waiting for humankind to return to Him. Such is the plague of the fifth bowl.

With *the sixth bowl*, the river Euphrates dries up. This prepares the way for armies to come from the east. Unclean spirits like frogs are seen coming out of the mouths of the dragon, the beast and the false prophet. These demonic spirits do signs and wonders. I believe they must do their false signs through wicked rulers who are yielded to them. Deceived people who are influenced by these spirits will follow these wicked rulers. There is such deception that the false rulers of this world believe the Devil is the one to be followed and that he can win against the Messiah and His armies! Even so, Pharaoh's troops followed the Israelites into the sea under the deception that they could defeat the people of God. This battle for which they are gathered is described in Zechariah 14 and Revelation 19. I believe the world will see Israel as the source of the problem and will falsely believe that if they destroy her, the plagues will cease and the supernatural power of the dragon will restore order. The world will see the battle in terms of supernatural power against supernatural power. However, they will be allied with the wrong power. This is an incredibly supernatural period of time.

So the armies of nations gather to the place called Armageddon. It is easy to see the potential of a world body such as the UN or some other alliance uniting the nations of the world in a unified military thrust. In a New Age religious orientation, the world will look at Evangelicals and Israelis as the two most narrow-minded peoples on the earth and as a roadblock to a world religion of maturity and the mutual affirmation of various pantheistic and polytheistic traditions. Once the believers in Jesus have been taken in the rapture, only Israel will be an impediment to their schemes.

The seventh bowl is the bowl of perfect completion. It is announced with the words, "It is done." There are thunderings, lightnings and a mighty earthquake (see Zechariah 14). The great city is divided into three parts and the cities of the nations fall in earthquakes. The Babylonian system receives the full wrath of God. So great is the judgment that it is thus described in apocalyptic symbolism: "Every island fled away, and the mountains were not found. And great hail from Heaven fell upon men...." (nuclear war? vs. 20-21a) In spite of all this, men blasphemed God. Only the final defeat of all the armies of the Antichrist will break the delusion. This is the theme of Revelation 19. The great city could be the center of the Babylonian system most closely represented by Rome in the first century. The city could also be Jerusalem, not yet submitted to Yeshua. We know from Zechariah 14 that a great earthquake will divide Jerusalem in the days of the last battle.

The Fall of Babylon (Rev. 18:21-19:10)

Revelation 18:21-24 gives another picture of the fall of the Babylonian system in terms of the fall of a city. A literal city may indeed fall, but the destruction of the whole system is the central issue.

As a millstone thrown into the sea, so will Babylon fall with violence. She shall be found no more. All the sounds of social life and industry will fully cease. The description is striking.

> *And the light of a lamp shall not shine in you anymore. And the voice of bridegroom and bride shall not be heard in you anymore. For your merchants were the great men of the earth, for by your sorcery all the nations were deceived. And in her was found the blood of prophets and saints, and of all who were slain on the earth.*
>
> Revelation 18:23-24

Chapter 19 begins with another picture of a great multitude in Heaven praising God and saying, "Salvation and glory and honor and power to the Lord our God!" He is praised for judging the great harlot and avenging the blood of His servants. The twenty-four elders again bow down and worship God. All are called upon to praise God.

In verses 7-9 we read of the announcement of the marriage of the Lamb, whose wife has made herself ready. We read, "And to her it was granted to be arrayed in fine linen, clean and bright, for *the fine linen is the righteous acts of the saints*... Blessed are those who are called to the marriage supper of the Lamb...These are the true sayings of God" (vs. 8-9). We see here the symbolic meaning of the white garments and perhaps of all priestly garments from ancient times.

The final defeat of the enemies of God leads to the feast of the marriage supper of the Lamb. I believe this marriage supper is the worldwide coronation ceremony of the King and His Bride, the Body of Believers. We are to be the ruling queen, standing at His side in the age to come.

When does this take place? After the wrath of God is complete all the nations who survive will repent (Zechariah 14). The judgments that take place between the Feast of Trumpets and the Day of Atonement lead to a Yom Kippur (Day of Atonement) repentance throughout the earth. Five days later comes the great Feast of Sukkot or Tabernacles (harvest). According to the Jewish calendar, Tishri 1 is the Feast of Trumpets; Tishri 10, the Day of Atonement, and Tishri 15, the Feast of Sukkot. The last is an eight-day celebration, the greatest celebration in the whole of ancient Israel's calendar. All nations will attend this feast. I believe it will be the marriage supper of the Lamb and His Bride. We are invited as part of the Bride. Israel and the others of all nations who survive come to witness the coronation. The defeat of the forces of the Antichrist rips away the veil of blindness over the nations. In the last invasion of Israel, this defeat is finalized. So we read in Isaiah 25:6-7.

And in this mountain the Lord of hosts will make for all people a feast of choice pieces...And He will destroy on this mountain the surface of the covering cast over all people, and the veil that is spread over all nations.

Many have speculated concerning the time of the marriage supper. Some have seen it as occurring during the first days after the rapture or during the seven years of the tribulation while the saints are in Heaven (a view we have already given reasons to reject). *I believe the symbolism of the fall feasts best fits with the marriage supper being part of the celebration of Sukkot.* This would align with the prophecy given in Zechariah 14 in that all nations send representatives to celebrate this feast in Israel. This feast would then be the annual anniversary celebration of the establishment of the rule of the Messiah and His Bride upon the earth. It would also be the annual memorial of the great wedding. We further see that the announcement of the wedding precedes the final victory described in Revelation 19:11-21.

The Return of Jesus with His Saints (Rev. 19:11-16)

In one of the most powerful passages in Scripture, John describes a vision of Heaven open. He sees One riding upon a white horse with the armies of Heaven, clothed in fine linen, white and clean, following Him. He is called "Faithful and True." "In righteousness He judges and makes war." We read also of the Messiah that:

His eyes were like a flame of fire, and on His head were many crowns. He had a name written that no one knew except Himself. He was clothed with a robe dipped in blood, and His name is called The Word of God...Out of His mouth goes a sharp sword, that with it He should strike the nations. And He Himself will rule them with a rod of iron. He Himself treads the winepress of the fierceness and wrath of Almighty God. And He has on His robe and on His thigh a name written, KING OF KINGS AND LORD OF LORDS.

Revelation 19:12-13, 15-16

This picture is also found in Isaiah 11, where we read that the Messiah will strike the earth with the rod from His mouth and with the breath of His lips He will slay the wicked (11:4).

The Defeat of the Antichrist and His Forces
(Rev. 19:17-21)

It seems incredible that the forces of the beast or the Antichrist would come against the awesome supernatural armies of God. Yet didn't Pharaoh pursue Israel into the sea despite the mighty signs and wonders that accompanied God's people? Indeed, the powers of the demonic hosts will be part of the deception that leads men to battle the Messiah. I believe Satan himself will be directly involved in this battle, will perhaps even be visible in this final conflagration. His appearing as an angel of light could be part of the world's reason for following him, the ultimate false god. I believe this last battle will see the veil lifted between the seen and the unseen worlds. We will see angelic and demonic hosts, Israel battling the earthly armies of the beast (Zech. 12:1-9), and at the same time the resurrected saints in supernatural bodies coming with the Lord.

At the time of battle, an angel invites the birds of the air to come to the feast of judgment. This is paralleled in Luke 17, "Wherever the body is, there the eagles will be gathered together" (v. 37).

The birds of prey are told they will eat the flesh of kings, captains, mighty men, horses, and of all kinds of people, free and slave, small and great.

The beast and the kings of the earth with their armies amazingly gather to make war against the Lord and His army. What utter deception! Does the Devil even deceive himself into believing he can win? I believe so. A more complete description of this battle with regard to the human armies which invade Israel is found in Zechariah 14. The armies of the Antichrist are therein described as coming under a plague; their flesh melts on their bodies and their eyes dissolve in their sockets. They are utterly routed, just as were the armies of Pharaoh.

The beast is captured, as is the false prophet who did the signs and wonders. They are cast into the lake of fire which burns with brimstone. We read that the rest of the armies are killed with the sword from Christ's mouth. When the final battle is engaged, there is no contest. The Messiah with His victorious saints prevails!

Satan Is Bound for 1000 Years (Rev. 20:1-3)

Of course, the defeat of the Antichrist must include the defeat of the Devil himself, the old dragon.

He empowered and inspired the beast. We read that an angel from Heaven has a key to the bottomless pit and a great chain to bind the Devil. He is given the power to lay hold of the dragon (the Devil) and to bind him for a thousand years in the bottomless pit. He is shut up with a seal on him, that he will no longer be able to deceive the nations. We will look at the question of his being loosed for a time after the thousand years later.

The great encouragement to us all is that *ultimate victory is assured*. We will see the defeat of the forces of evil; we will join in the marriage supper of the Lamb and we will see the full establishment of the Kingdom of God!

CHAPTER VII

ENTRY INTO THE PROMISED LAND!

Revelation 20:4-22:21 pictures us entering into the Age to Come and reveals the conditions of that age. Again, the foreshadowing in the Mosaic writings is very strong. After Israel received the Law, they were to defeat the enemies of God and take possession of the promised land, a type of the Age to Come. The battles in taking the land are types of the battles of the last days before entering into the land. Had Moses and the Israelites not sinned, Moses himself would have led the Israelites into the promised land. Due to Moses' sin, Joshua (Yeshua—the same name as Jesus!) became the leader of the "entering in." Due to the sin of unbelief in the Israelites, the crossing over took place forty years later than expected.

The Millennial Age and the Last Rebellion
(Rev. 20:4-10)

Great controversy rages concerning the meaning of Revelation 20:4-10. A straightforward reading of this passage indicates a resurrection of the dead, initiating a 1000-year period of peace under the rulership of the Messiah. The dead mentioned in this passage are only those who had been beheaded for their witness to Jesus and who did not worship the beast or receive his mark. This is the first resurrection. Over these death has no power, but they are called priests with God and reign with the Messiah for a thousand years.

Most interpreters believe the resurrection spoken of is not limited to the martyrs of the last days, even though that is who John saw. This is because First Corinthians 15 and First Thessalonians 4:16-17 seem to indicate a resurrection of all the saved at the time of the return of Jesus. In every age there is an opportunity for people to give themselves to the world, the flesh and the Devil. Only those who do not do so are resurrected.

After this thousand-year period we read of Satan being loosed to deceive the nations again. A vast multitude, as the sand of the sea, goes up to the camp of the saints and the beloved city (Jerusalem?). However, a fire comes forth from God and devours them. The Devil is cast into the lake of fire, which leads to the great white throne judgment (Rev. 20:11-15).

The amillennial interpretation of this passage has held sway throughout most of Church history. This interpretation views Revelation 20:1-10 as simply recounting the content of the early chapters in a different way. Augustine, in the fifth century, was a great proponent of this viewpoint. Basically, it was thought that the end of Roman opposition to the Church produced a situation in which Satan was bound. This binding was thought to be the condition of most of this age. The first resurrection is viewed as the experience of being born again. Those who were born again and died are alive in Heaven and are reigning in heaven with the Messiah. The fulness of receiving our permanent resurrection bodies, however, was thought to await the Lord's return at the end of the 1000 years. Ultimately it was taught that all of the saved and lost would be judged at one time at the end of the 1000-year period. This 1000-year period is seen as symbolic of the time frame between the first and second comings of Jesus. The number "1000" is 10 X 10 X 10, which is God's complete order for this age. The end of this age manifests the great rebellion against God and His people. This is seen as the same rebellion as is described throughout the book in different ways. The defeat is seen as the same as that depicted in Revelation 19. After this age comes the return of Jesus, the judgment and the New Heavens and Earth. No earthly Millennial Age is expected in the future; hence the name "Amillennial" or "Present Millennial" to describe this view.

The Amillennialist never tires of pointing out how foolish it seems to him to believe in an age in which earthly nations continue while the resurrected rule and live side by side with the non-resurrected. For him, the passages in the Hebrew Scriptures concerning a worldwide commonwealth under the capital of Jerusalem, with Israel being the chief nation among the nations, is wooden literalism. He believes that the picture in the prophets of a glorious age on earth with humankind living in prosperity, propagating children and dying at ripe old ages, is symbolic. Yet there is nothing in the Hebrew Scriptures to indicate that this is symbolic; indeed, the ancients understood the difference between living for a long time and then dying and living forever (e.g., the meaning of the tree of life giving everlasting life in the Garden of Eden). The blessings of Israel in the classical amillennial scheme are interpreted as referring to the Church. Again, there is nothing in the Hebrew text to indicate that this is so.

My view of Revelation 20:4-10 follows what is known as the Pre-Millennial view. I believe there are two stages to the Age to Come, or entering into the promised land. The first stage is the Millennial Age, which is established after the return of Jesus. The second stage is the coming of the New Heavens and New Earth, which takes place after the great white throne judgment.

What is the nature of the Millennial Age? How do we interpret the first and second resurrections in Revelation 20, and why is there a Millennial stage to entering the promised land? I believe we can answer these questions with prayerful reflection.

Although the Millennial Age is a glorious age of peace and prosperity in which all nations are unified under the rulership of the Messiah, it is not the state of perfection. Even the glorious description in the prophets describes an age in which death still ultimately claims the lives of earthly humankind. However, the human race lives to great old age. The Millennial Age serves several purposes.

First, I believe God works through a restoration process whereby the effects of the fall are reversed, somewhat like a movie running backward. The Millennium is the restoration of pre-flood longevity. During the pre-flood period, man lived for over 900 years. So in the Millennium, Isaiah says that one who dies at 100 years will be considered to be under a curse (Isa. 65:20). In reversing the curse, that stage of human longevity is to be recovered.

Secondly, with Satan bound, I believe man will be able to fully live out the principles of faith, healing and prosperity promised in the Law. This will be a worldwide condition. All God's Laws (principles) and promises will be found to be fully effective in an earthly state. Of course, human ability will be the result of faith and the power of the Spirit. I believe God wants to demonstrate His truth in a special way during this age. This will be remembered throughout eternal ages.

The first resurrection would be the resurrection of the saints who are the ruling Bride or queen at the side of Jesus. I see nothing ludicrous in the resurrected ruling the non-resurrected. That the two types of humans can have interchange on this earth is no more strange than the interchange between humans and angels or between the resurrected Messiah and His disciples during the forty days between His resurrection and His ascension. Indeed, this forty-day period may be a foreshadowing of the Millennial Age. Those in the first resurrection have overcome; the second death has no power over them. The second death is the everlasting separation from God that takes place after the final judgment. It is consignment to the lake of fire.

In Revelation 20:7-9 we read of the last great rebellion. How can this be possible if the resurrected are ruling and if the world has experienced peace and prosperity under the beneficent rule of the Messiah?

God has to test the generations born during the latter part of this age. By the end of the Millennium, all those who survived to enter this age will have passed away. I do not believe Jesus and the resurrected saints will throughout this age be localized in specific places on earth as they rule. Will Jesus rule in Jerusalem on a literal throne? I believe He will certainly and regularly appear there. However, Jesus and the saints, I believe, will have access to Heaven and earth. As the Millennial Age continues, the rule with a rod of iron of the Messiah and His saints will be less and less dominant. We will transfer more and more rule and authority to humans still in their earthly bodies. Israel will have a major role in this rulership. Satan's being loosed implies that the power of deception will be loosed. A situation will have to arise to test the nations of the world whereby those without true hearts can be deceived. It will look as though God's designated rulers are in the wrong and are to be overthrown. This is similar to the way the Israelites rebelled against Moses when he was absent and upon Sinai.

This rebellion produces no drawn-out period as in the tribulation of the last days. Once the hearts are tested, the judgment is swift. The Devil is judged and sent to his eternal doom.

For the most part, however, the Millennial Age is such a glorious age of the Spirit that I believe it to be an age of promise paralleling Israel's entering into the promised land. All nations will celebrate the biblical feasts unto Jesus, the knowledge of the Lord will cover the earth as the water covers the beds of the seas and all flesh will know the reality of the Spirit in the first part of that Age (Joel 2:28, Isa. 45:22-25, Zech. 14:9, Isa. 65:20-25, Isa.

66:23). In this age all the promises to regather the Jewish people and to make Israel a praise to the whole earth will be fulfilled. However, the everlasting age which follows the Millennial Age, the New Heavens and Earth, is the promised land *par excellence*.

The Great White Throne Judgment (Rev. 20:11-15)

The great white throne provides an image of God's final judgment before the New Heavens and New Earth. All the dead not previously resurrected are alive at this time. This judgment is for the lost from all ages before the Millennial Age and for the saved and lost who died during that age. I believe it is a clear implication of Revelation 20:12 that some of those who appear before the throne of God are saved; their names are found in the Book of Life. The section is beyond literal human understanding as it says that death and hades were cast into the lake of fire. This simply means that death and hades are finally and forever destroyed from the society of the redeemed.

Those whose names are not found written in the Book of Life are cast into the lake of fire. That lake seems to be a place of destruction, but not of total destruction (suffering the full experience of the results of human self-centeredness and separation from God).

The New Heaven and New Earth (Rev. 21:1-8)

Some debate whether the New Heavens and New Earth are a total renewal of this creation or a completely new creation. However it is looked at, can we not simply agree that what God will do for us will be most wonderful? We will live in the reality of a universe that is fully freed from the bondage of corruption and decay.

John also sees a New Jerusalem coming down from Heaven as a bride adorned for her husband (v. 2). Is the New Jerusalem the people of God or the dwelling place of the people of God? I believe it is both. God now includes within the Bride of Messiah the saved from all ages. The great promise of the prophets is now fulfilled, that God abides with His people forever.

> *Behold, the tabernacle of God is with men, and He will dwell with them, and they shall be His people, and God Himself will be with them and be their God. And God will wipe away every tear from their eyes; there shall be no more death, nor sorrow, nor crying; and there shall be no more pain, for the former things have passed away.*
>
> Revelation 21:3-4

What words can possibly be added to this glorious expression? The Beginning and the End, the Alpha and the Omega, makes all things new. He gives the water of life freely to all who will drink of it. We who overcome will be children of God forever. He will dwell with us and in us as His own Tabernacle. However, as we read in verse 6, all the wicked will be excluded.

The New Jerusalem (Rev. 21:9-21)

A wonderful account is given in this passage of the New Jerusalem descending. It is so wonderful that the reader should certainly read the passage first and allow for its direct impact before he reads our only too inadequate comments. However, there are a few things that are worth emphasizing.

The New Jerusalem is both the people and the center of the order of God in the Age to Come. God dwells in the midst of His people, hence, in the midst of the New Jerusalem. We and the city are the Temple of God in the Age to Come. Where the literal and the symbolic divide we cannot tell. This passage strains at realities that are difficult for us mortals to comprehend.

The walls of the city are great and high with twelve gates. Angels are over each gate, giving a picture of majesty. Each gate has upon it the names of the twelve tribes of the children of Israel. In the Torah, God said His Name would forever be "The God of Abraham, Isaac and Jacob." Our faith is rooted in Israel, and from Jewish people this faith was spread to the world. God will yet fully recover the meaning of Israel and restore this nation to the one olive tree of God (Rom. 11:24-29). God will redeem all that is truly good. It is indeed significant, therefore, that God forever will identify the New Jerusalem with the Israelite roots of redemptive history.

Out of Israel came the twelve apostles. Hence, the foundations of the walls have upon them the names of the apostles. The faith is thus represented by its great historic foundations in the apostles, but also stretches back beyond this to the twelve patriarchs.

The city is like a huge cube with its width and its length given as 12,000 furlongs. This is 1,380 miles! The dimensions are again symbolic, twelve being the number of Israel and the people of God. The walls' measurement of 144 cubits is a multiple of 12. Again, this is the dwelling of the people of God.

Gold is the royal metal, the predominant material in the New Jerusalem. There are also many varieties of precious stones. Each of the twelve foundations has its own precious gems of decor. The gates are made of pearl, from which we derive the expression, "the pearly gates." There are twelve such gates.

Beyond all these descriptions of glory is the fact that the glory of God illumines the city, and He dwells in it. The Lamb as well is its light. The gates are forever open; all the saved walk in this light forever. The kings (rulers) of all the nations, who are part of the New Heavens and New Earth, bring their glory into it. No corruption shall ever defile it. It will be forever open to all whose names are recorded in the Lamb's Book of Life.

The River of Life: Paradise Restored (Rev. 22:1-5)

The river of the water of life, clear as crystal, comes forth from the throne of God. Indeed, the water of life is found in our drinking deeply of our relationship with God. This is life! On the banks of the river are twelve trees of life bearing twelve fruits. This is the food for the people of God. Whereas Adam and Eve were banned from paradise and the Tree of Life in the Garden of Eden, now mankind is restored to paradise. However, it is a better paradise than was ever lost. The leaves of the trees heal the nations. In other words, the life that comes from God will provide total and everlasting healing.

The curse is ended; the throne of God and the Lamb are in the midst of the City of God and His servants will serve and dwell with God. How wonderful are these words:

*They shall see His face, and His name shall be on
their foreheads. And there shall be no night there.
They need no lamp nor light of the sun, for the Lord
God gives them light. And they shall reign forever
and ever.*

Revelation 22:4-5

Closing Exhortations and Warnings (Rev. 22:6-21)

The closing makes it clear that for the people of God,
the end of this age is forever on the doorstep. It could all
come about very quickly. The Lamb of God can say, **"Behold, I am coming quickly! Blessed is he who keeps the
words of the prophecy of this book"** (22:7).

How does one "keep" the words of such a prophecy?
They are kept by holy, fruitful Kingdom living. They are
kept by understanding the forces of evil and doing
spiritual warfare, having the certainty of ultimate victory. We rescue the lost and serve, that believers might
be whole. We need to recognize the forces of the an-
tichrists that are already in the world. We must resist the
lure of Babylon, which is a spiritual reality in every
period of this transitional age. "The time is near" (v. 10).
A time of division is coming wherein the holy and the
unholy, the just and the unjust, the righteous and the fil-
thy will fully manifest the extremes of good and evil
before the great day of the return of the Lord.

The Lord, who comes quickly, will bring His reward.
We shall receive the fruit of our lives that will last. The
separation that is coming upon the earth will lead to the
everlasting separation. Those who keep God's commandments have the right to the Tree of Life and access
to the gates of the city. However, outside the Kingdom

of God will dwell all the unrighteous, **"dogs and sorcerers, and sexually immoral and murderers and idolaters, and whoever loves and practices a lie."**

The everlasting Messiah is now forever a human being, since He was born of the house of David. He is not only the Angel of the Covenant in the Hebrew Scriptures, the divine Son of the Triune Godhead, but is as well the Root and Offspring of David. He is the Bright and Morning Star.

The water of life is not only available in the Age to Come. It is available now to those who will fully yield their lives to His Lordship and the joy of walking with Him. Hence, as in Isaiah 55 and John 7, we read of the invitation to come and drink of the water of life freely.

The book of this prophecy is to be carefully preserved and not tampered with. Indeed, this is a warning to us to carefully handle the Word of God with great reverence concerning its intended meaning! We must not take away from or add to the Word of God. The penalty for violating this prophecy is the loss of everlasting life in the Holy City of God.

How amazing and wonderful! The Bible begins with paradise lost. It ends with a greater paradise restored that can never again be lost. The promised land of the New Heavens and the New Earth is ours after all of the foreshadowing exodus events and lands of promise are past. We have seen the exodus from Egypt and the promised land of ancient Israel; the exodus of the pilgrims and the puritans to the promised land of America, the great missionary base for the 20th century; the exodus of Jews from the nations back to their ancient promised land as part of God's last days preparation; and we will yet see the exodus of God's people into the

glory cloud which will lead to the promised land of the
Millennial Age. However, all will end in that glorious
promised land of the New Heavens and New Earth with
its New Jerusalem, where God will dwell in the midst of
His people and wipe away every tear. We will live in joy-
ful, loving community with God and His people forever!
This is *the* sustaining hope in times of trial and the destiny of God's holy people. We close with the words en-
ding the book itself:

> *He who testifies to these things says, "Surely I am*
> *coming quickly." Amen. Even so, come, Lord Jesus!*
> *The grace of our Lord Jesus Christ be with you all.*
> *Amen.*

APPENDIX I

NUMBERS IN REVELATION

People's ability to make much of every number in the Bible is extraordinary. Most people who engage in a heavy emphasis on biblical numerology are simply unaware of how tenuous their seemingly coherent schemes are. This was made clear in the fiasco of 1988, when teachers claimed that Jesus was returning on Rosh Hashana (in September) of 1988 according to their calculations. There are many possible interpretations of numbers, age-day schemes, week-day schemes and others. "1290 days" is taken to mean 1290 *years* in some historical views.

However, having spoken these cautions, there are some numbers that seem to have clear symbolic meaning while possibly being more literal in ultimate fulfillment.

The following numbers and multiples of numbers are usually seen by Bible scholars as having the following meanings. Biblical usage and intertestamental usage in ancient Jewish writings confirm these meanings.

3: This is the number representing the Godhead, the triune God.

6: This is the number of man, who was created on the sixth day of creation. It can refer to man's self-sufficiency without God.

7: The number of perfection. The world was created in seven days. Rest is commanded on the seventh day. There are seven branches to the light of the holy lampstand. As the number of trumpets in Revelation it implies a seven-year time span, one for each trumpet blast, from one feast to the next (a possibility set forth by Pastor Keith Intrater).

8: The day of resurrection; new beginnings.

10: This is the number of completion. It includes the ten plagues on Egypt, 1/10 being the tithe, 10 being the number representing the confederacy against God in the last days.

12: The number of the tribes of Israel or the people of God. Note also that there were twelve apostles; their names and the names of the twelve tribes are inscribed on the gates and foundation stones of the New Jerusalem.

24: Twice the number of the people of God; possibly Israel and the Church together represented by the 24 elders in heaven.

70: The number of the nations from the table of the nations found in Genesis 10 and the sacrifices for the nations during the feast of Tabernacles in the Book of Numbers. 70 is a multiple of perfection and completeness (7 X 10).

144,000: This is the number of the sealed. It is a multiple of 12s and 10s, a complete number of God's sealed ones.

666: The false trinity of human power and exaltation (six three times); the Antichrist.

1260: Days of judgment; approximately three and one half years. 1260 represents half a measure of perfect judgment because of God's mercy in shortening the days (Rev. 11:3).

I trust this brief summary is helpful to the reader.

APPENDIX II

THE TIME FRAME

by Keith Intrater

There are two passages tucked away in Leviticus that have a surprising impact on our understanding of how the biblical feasts foreshadow end-times prophecy. The first passage is the following:

When you come into the land which I give to you, and reap its harvest, then you shall bring a sheaf of the firstfruits of your harvest to the priest. He shall wave the sheaf before the Lord, to be accepted on your behalf; on the day after the Sabbath the priest shall wave it.

Leviticus 23:10b-11

This describes the Feast of First Fruits, which takes place on the first day of the week (i.e. Sunday) after Passover. It was on the first day of the week after Passover that Jesus was raised from the dead. Jesus is called the *"first fruits from the dead"* (I Cor. 15:20, 23).

Jesus was resurrected on the day of the Feast of First Fruits. The resurrection of Jesus fulfilled that feast, and the feast of First Fruits prophesied the resurrection of Jesus.

Jesus was crucified on Passover. He was raised from the dead on the day of the Fast of First Fruits. The Holy Spirit was poured out on the Feast of Pentecost (Shavuot, Weeks). All three events were fulfilled in the same year. The events surrounding the birth of the Church were predicted in the Old Testament feasts. The feasts and their prophetic fulfillment all came to pass in the same year.

The biblical feasts are arranged in two groups: spring feasts and fall feasts. The spring feasts have to do with the events of the first century and have already been fulfilled. The fall feasts have to do with end-times prophecies and have not yet been fulfilled.

If the biblical pattern holds true, we can expect the end-times prophecies to be fulfilled on the days of the feasts that foreshadow them. The Feast of Trumpets relates to the trumpets in the Book of Revelation. The Day of Atonement relates to repentance in Israel at the time of Armageddon (Zech. 12:10, ff). The Feast of Tabernacles relates to the inaugural celebration of the Messianic Kingdom. Together, the fall feasts foreshadow the second coming of Jesus.

The second pertinent passage from Leviticus is 25:8-10a.

*And you shall count seven sabbaths of years for your-
self, seven times seven years; and the time of the
seven sabbaths of years shall be to you forty-nine
years. Then you shall cause the trumpet of the Jubilee
to sound on the tenth day of the seventh month; on
the Day of Atonement you shall make the trumpet to
sound throughout all your land. And you shall con-
secrate the fiftieth year, and proclaim liberty
throughout the land to all its inhabitants. It shall be
a Jubilee for you.*

The Book of Revelation contains three series of judgments. The first series comprises seven seals, the second
series seven trumpets, and the third seven bowls. The
seven seals are guarding a scroll by keeping it closed.
The seals must be opened in order to read the scroll,
which contains the remainder of the prophecies for the
end times.

The seven seals are seven preparatory stages leading
to the end-times events recorded in the scroll. Each seal
opened brings us closer to the trumpets and bowls. If the
seven seals lead up to the events recorded in the scroll,
they may be seen as encompassing longer periods of
time that span Church history. The history of the
Church is encapsulated in the descriptions of the seven
seals.

The seven trumpets represent seven Feasts of Trumpets. The blowing of a trumpet signified the entrance of
the king and his retinue. The Feast of Trumpets therefore
rightly symbolizes the return of Jesus as conquering King.
The Feast of Trumpets occurs once each year. It would be
consistent with the biblical pattern for the seven trumpets
to cover a seven-year period—one year for each Feast of

Trumpets. The time frame in the Book of Revelation speeds up as the judgments come closer to an end.

The seven trumpets are followed by seven bowls. This is the most intense time of wrath and warfare. The final conflict between God and the nations comes to a head. The seven bowls of wrath take place in a relatively short period of time. The Feast of Trumpets takes place on the first day of the seventh month. The day of Atonement takes place on the tenth day. If the seventh trumpet of Revelation is blown on the Feast of Trumpets, and if the day of Atonement trumpet announces the start of the Jubilee age, there are approximately ten days in which those cataclysmic events of final judgment will take place.

It is interesting that the Jewish rabbis refer to the ten days between Rosh HaShannah and Yom Kippur as "The Ten Days of Awe." Let us recall that the events surrounding the death and resurrection of Jesus all took place in the same year on the exact days of the feast foreshadowing them.

We will better understand the timing of events in the Book of Revelation if we recognize that the seven seals cover an extended period of time leading up to the final conflicts, the seven trumpets take place during the span of seven yearly Feasts of Trumpets, and the seven bowls of wrath will be fulfilled rapidly in the last year of this present age.

APPENDIX III

CHART OUTLINE

by Dan Juster

The Last of the Last Days: Revelation and Other Passages

1 Thes. 4:16
1 Cor. 15:51 ff

Rev. 12 History of Israel and the church	7 SEALS	7 TRUMPETS	7 BOWLS OF WRATH (Tishri 1) — 10 DAYS	YOM KIPPUR (Tishri 10) — 5 DAYS	SUCCOT (Tishri 15)
	Indefinite longer period of time	7 Years of successive Feasts of Trumpets	The seventh shofar, rapture and resurrection Rev. 14	Saints return with Jesus and defeat Anti-christ	Tabernacles marriage supper: King and Queen (bride) Zech. 14
	Wars, famine, environmental problems	Church in great unity Jn. 17:21	Preceded by Israel's Confession Matt. 23:39	Defeat Devil Bowls of wrath He treads wine press of God Zech. 14:3 ff	All nations come to celebrate feast
	Martyrs Rev.5	Restoration of prophets—esp. 2 Like Moses and Aaron Rev. 11 / Excursus	Context: invasion Zech. 14:1,2 Rev. 19	Yom Kippur Nations and Israel repent cleansed Zech. 12:10 13:1 Rev. 1:7	
	144,000 Rev. 7 Israeli Messianic Jews sealed	Revelation of Anti-christ Rev. 13 / Excursus	Exodus into glory cloud		
	Rev. 7 multitude from all nation saved	Babylon and Harlot Rev. 17,18 Excursus	Exodus from Jerusalem under seige		
	Ezek. 38,39 invasion				

TIKKUN MINISTRIES

Tikkun is a Hebrew term that means *restoration*. It reflects our burden and belief. We believe Scripture teaches that the Church will be restored to power, love, unity and righteousness. This renewal will be a key to the restoration of the Jewish people and their ingrafting into *"her own olive tree"* (Romans 11). We believe that the last days, according to Scripture, will see a progression of events leading toward the full restoration of Israel and the Church. As the Church is restored, we will see a significant number of Jews saved and a continued return of Jews to Israel. With those Jews who are the saved remnant of Israel, the Church will intercede and witness in love until Israel turns to Yeshua. Romans 11 is a key passage of last days teaching. Tikkun Ministries is committed to seeing these restorations come to pass in the last days.

As part of our vision we are engaged in the following ministries:

1. Training, sending out and supporting congregational planters in the United States, Israel and other countries.

2. Fostering Jewish ministry in local churches.

3. A full-time Bible and graduate School for training leaders for the Jewish vineyard and for work in the Church.

4. Sending out teachers and preachers for conferences, evangelistic campaigns, services in Messianic congregations and churches, etc.

5. Sponsoring music and dance ministries.

6. Helping to bring about a consistent pattern of unity with the Body as an expression of our deep conviction.

The leaders available for the above ministries include Daniel Juster, who is the Chairman of the Board of Tikkun Ministries and Messiah Biblical Institute, head pastor of Beth Messiah Congregation, and an author. Michael Brown is Dean of Messiah Biblical Institute, an author, teacher and revivalist. Keith Intrater is pastor of El Shaddai Congregation, a Tikkun board member, an author and teacher. Andrew Shishkoff is also a pastor at Beth Messiah Congregation, a Tikkun board member and an evangelist. Jerry Miller is a pastor at Beth Messiah Congregation, a Tikkun board member and a teacher. Mikhael Murnane is the Director of Jerusalem Worship Dance, overseen by Tikkun board members.

The following pages list books available by our Tikkun leaders. Please use the form at the back of this book to place your order.

LAST DAYS TRILOGY

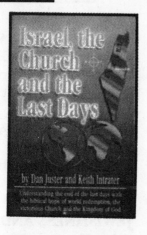

ISRAEL, THE CHURCH AND THE LAST DAYS
Must reading for all believers who want an exciting new perspective on the last days and the end-time role of Israel and the Church.
Price $9.95

FROM IRAQ TO ARMAGEDDON
This book gives an in-depth analysis of end-time prophecy concerning the Middle East.
Price $7.95

REVELATION: THE PASSOVER KEY
An intriguing analysis explaining the similarities of the exodus from Egypt to the end times.
Price $7.95

MESSIANIC JEWISH THEMES

JEWISH ROOTS, A FOUNDATION
OF BIBLICAL THEOLOGY
A significant book on Messianic Judaism which offers insight on many difficult questions.   **$10.00**

GROWING TO MATURITY, A MESSIANIC
JEWISH GUIDE
This book is used by many congregations for membership classes.   **$9.00**

JEWISHNESS AND JESUS
A booklet to help you share Messiah with your unsaved Jewish friends.   **$1.00**

OUR HANDS ARE STAINED WITH BLOOD
For 1500 years the Church has persecuted the Jewish people. This shocking book exposes the roots of Christian anti-Semitism.   **$7.95**

OTHER BOOKS BY OUR AUTHORS

MICHAEL BROWN

HOW SAVED ARE WE?
An eye-opening book that will forever change our perspective on what it means to be a disciple of the Lord.
$6.00

THE END OF THE AMERICAN
GOSPEL ENTERPRISE

This urgent call for repentance exposes the bankrupt state of the American Church—and shows us the way to a real outpouring. **$6.00**

WHATEVER HAPPENED
TO THE POWER OF GOD?

This stirring book asks the questions you have always wanted to ask, and confronts you with answers that could change your life. **$7.95**

KEITH INTRATER

THE APPLE OF HIS EYE

Find out how your life can be transformed as you are bathed in the light of God's grace. **$6.00**

COVENANT RELATIONSHIPS

A handbook on the biblical principles of integrity and loyalty. This book lays important foundations for congregational health and right spiritual attitudes. **$12.00**

DAN JUSTER

DYNAMICS OF SPIRITUAL DECEPTION

This book will help you to avoid demonic counterfeit in Spirit-filled congregations. **$ 4.00**

ORDER FORM

NAME_____ PHONE_____

ADDRESS_____

_____

All items available to ministries and bookstores, in quantities of 5 or more, at 40% discount.

All orders must be prepaid.

PLEASE TURN OVER THIS ORDER FORM AND FILL OUT THE FOLLOWING FOR EACH BOOK ORDER:

1. The item number

2. The cost of the book

3. The number of that item you would like to order.

4. The amount of each item

5. The totals and the amount enclosed.